SERIES

GUIDE FOR MUSIC MINISTERS

THIRD EDITION

Jennifer Kerr Budziak

Christopher J. Ferraro

Corinna Laughlin

Paul Turner

Nihil Obstat
Rev. Mr. Daniel G. Welter, JD
Chancellor
Archdiocese of Chicago
April 29, 2021

Imprimatur
Most Rev. Robert G. Casey
Vicar General
Archdiocese of Chicago
April 29, 2021

The *Nihil Obstat* and *Imprimatur* are official declarations that a book is free of doctrinal and moral error. No implication is contained therein that those who have granted the *Nihil Obstat* and *Imprimatur* agree with the content, opinions, or statements expressed. Nor do they assume any legal responsibility associated with publication.

The Glossary definitions and portions of the Resources section were written by Dennis C. Smolarski, SJ, and Joseph DeGrocco. Music engraved by James T. Gerber.

Cover photo by John Zich. The photo on page 61 © Liturgy Training Publications; photos on pages 2, 5, 10, 12, 24, and 41 are by John Zich; the images on pages 16 and 18 are courtesy Wikimedia Commons.

This book was edited by Danielle A. Noe. Michael A. Dodd was the production editor, Anna Manhart was the designer, and Juan Alberto Castillo was the production artist.

This book is part of the Liturgical Ministry Series®.

25 24 23 22 21   1 2 3 4 5

Printed in the United States of America

Library of Congress Control Number: 2021936116

ISBN 978-1-61671-583-0

ELMM3

Contents

Preface

"We played the flute for you, but you did not dance,
we sang a dirge but you did not mourn."

—Matthew 11:17

Jesus was not very happy about the music. He shouted at the musicians and told them to go away.

Now, Jesus liked music. And he loved everyone. He taught us to love our enemies. So surely he loved musicians.

In fact, shortly after this embarrassing incident with musicians (they were flute players, by the way), he softened up. He compared himself with flute players. He was complaining to the crowds that they were not responding to his words, just as they had not responded to John the Baptist.

They reminded him of children at play. Children played flutes, encouraging others to dance in joy as at a wedding. They also sang dirges to get others to mourn as at a funeral. These were games of make-believe. Well, one day Jesus probably watched children play flutes when no one danced. So they tried singing, but no one mourned either. The children became frustrated. No matter what game they played, no one joined in.[1]

Jesus knew the feeling. If John the Baptist was like children who sing dirges, Jesus was like children who play flutes. There were people who heard John and did not follow, and then they heard Jesus but did not follow him either. Jesus was exasperated. "To what shall I compare this generation?" he wondered. "Children."[2]

So, Jesus knew the power of music, and he compared himself to children skilled at the flute. He believed that music had a purpose that went beyond the player. It involved other people in its lure and charm.

All things being equal, then, Jesus had no problem with flute players. He loved flute players.

But he was unhappy with this particular group of flute players. Jesus had been speaking to some people when an official interrupted him with this sad news: "My daughter has just died."[3] The official immediately followed up this report with a request. "Come, lay your hand on her, and she will live."[4]

1. See Matthew 11:16–19.
2. Matthew 11:16.
3. Matthew 9:18.
4. Matthew 9:18.

So Jesus dropped everything and followed him. Here was a twist. Usually it is disciples who drop everything to follow Jesus. Here, it is Jesus, and the disciples followed. They were led to a place where the power of God was to be revealed.

But before they got there, Jesus was interrupted again. A woman who had been suffering hemorrhages for twelve years touched the tassel on his cloak. It was enough for Jesus to notice. He noticed not just the touch, but the faith in the woman's heart. "Courage, daughter!"[5] he said. "Your faith has saved you."[6] The woman was cured. But the real story was deeper than that. Her faith had saved her.

When Jesus finally arrived at the official's house, he started giving orders. After all, things had not gone his way lately. His talk had been interrupted. He set out on an unexpected journey. A woman practically stole a physical cure from him.

He had work to do now. It was not a good time to play the flute. But there they were. Word had gotten out that the little girl had died, so the family started arranging the funeral customs. They called in the flute players. The crowd was making a commotion. Jesus sized up the scene and declared the whole business inappropriate.

"Go away!" he said. "The girl is not dead but sleeping."[7] If all this had annoyed Jesus, the crowd just made it worse. They ridiculed him. Jesus finally managed to get the whole crowd outside—together with the flute players.

He took the girl by the hand and she arose.[8]

Now, there was something to play music for.

—Paul Turner

5. Matthew 9:22.
6. Matthew 9:22.
7. See Matthew 9:24.
8. See Matthew 9:18–26.

How to Use This Resource

As a music minister, you are offering your gift to the glory of God. You are no faithless flute player, staring at the dead as at just another job. You are filled with faith, a faith that saves. You are filled with life, filled with song, and filled with discipleship. Where Jesus leads, you will follow. You will play and sing what fits the occasion. You will lead others to Christ.

Within the Mass, the music serves a variety of needs. It gathers the voices of the assembly into one. It accompanies processions. It invites people to listen. It colors and drives the drama of worship.

Whether you sing or play, your ministry is essential to the worship of your parish. Your skill will disclose your faith. Your faith will attract the faith of others. God will be praised.

This book will tell you why we have music during Mass and how it developed. It will explain how your role fits within the overall pattern of the liturgy. It will answer some of your basic questions about the music during Mass. And it will help form your spiritual life, so that your music may explore more deeply the mystery of God.

About the Authors

Jennifer Kerr Budziak is a Chicago-area conductor, author, mezzo-soprano, and composer and is a frequent clinician in the area of musical formation, ritual and theology, and choral techniques at workshops nationwide. Dr. Budziak holds degrees in choral conducting from Northwestern University and Indiana University. Her ACS award-winning book *Sowing Seeds, Bearing Fruit*, a process for growing an engaged and singing assembly, was published in 2012. She is a contributing author of *Guide for Cantors, Third Edition* with Liturgy Training Publications, and she authored *Sight-Sing a New Song* (2005), a textbook on sight-singing and music notation for beginners, among other volumes on liturgy and music. Her compositions for adult and children's choirs can be found in the catalogs of GIA Publications, World Library Publications (now part of GIA), and Oregon Catholic Press. She has served on the Council of the National Association of Pastoral Musicians and is a frequent presenter at the organization's regional and national conferences. Dr. Budziak has served on the faculties of Loyola University of Chicago, North Central College, Concordia University, St. Xavier University, and the Catholic Theological Union. She currently serves NPM as the editor of *Pastoral Music* magazine.

Christopher J. Ferraro is director of music at Our Lady of Perpetual Help Church, Lindenhurst, New York. He also directs the Liturgical Music Institute at the Seminary of the Immaculate Conception, Huntington, New York, and is a member of the diocesan liturgical commission for the Diocese of Rockville Centre. He serves on the board of directors for the Federation of Diocesan Liturgical Commissions and is a member of the NPM council. Chris holds master's degrees in theology and pastoral studies as well as an advanced certificate in pastoral liturgy from the Seminary of the Immaculate Conception, Huntington, New York, and is certified as director of worship through the Alliance for the Certification for Lay Ecclesial Ministers.

Corinna Laughlin is the pastoral assistant for liturgy at St. James Cathedral in Seattle, Washington, and liturgy consultant for the Archdiocese of Seattle. She has written extensively on the liturgy for Liturgy Training Publications and has contributed to *Pastoral Liturgy®*, *Ministry and Liturgy*, and other publications. She holds a doctorate in English from the University of Washington.

Paul Turner is the pastor of the Cathedral of the Immaculate Conception in Kansas City, Missouri, and the director of the Office of Divine Worship for the Diocese of Kansas City–St. Joseph. He holds a doctorate in sacred theology from Sant'Anselmo in Rome and is the author of many pastoral and theological resources. He serves as a facilitator for the International Commission on English in the Liturgy.

Questions for Discussion and Reflection

1. Why have you agreed to serve as a music minister?
2. What do you hope to gain in your understanding of the theology and function of the ministry through this book?
3. How is making music a spiritual experience for you?

Chapter One

Your Ministry and the Liturgy

[The liturgy] is the source and summit of the Christian life.

—*Lumen gentium*, 11

The Letter to the Ephesians beautifully encourages the spirituality of music ministers with this advice: "[B]e filled with the Spirit, addressing one another [in] psalms and hymns and spiritual songs, singing and playing to the Lord in your hearts, giving thanks always and for everything in the name of our Lord Jesus Christ to God the Father."[1] According to this passage Christian music has an external and an internal function. It is used in public worship as a way that we express our faith to one another. And it awakens a personal faith, in which we sing and play to God in our hearts. Music helps us give God thanks at all times for all things in the name of Jesus Christ. We do it in public and in private.

You carry songs in your head. At different times of the day, you will remember one of them. Sometimes you hear the same song over and over; you can't get rid of it. Other times you may be surprised by the song you suddenly remember from long ago or from some forgotten source. In any case, the music is in you. It plays you. You hum it in private, but you sing and play it in public. In music you address other people, and when you are not performing it, you keep it in your heart.

Whenever you sing or play music at church, you exercise something beyond your skills: you exercise your faith. When you pray the Rosary, you say words and move beads, but you center your heart in prayer. When you read Scripture, you read words, but you center your heart in the One who inspired them. When you sing and play at church, your heart should be centered on prayer. Become aware of the presence of God around you and within you. When you make music, know that it is God with whom you resonate.

Your ministry is an essential part of the Church's worship. It will serve the flow of liturgical prayer. It will add beauty and artistry to the way people pray. It will enliven the words that express belief and immerse those who sing them into the mystery of God. You are the one with a skill to sing and to play instruments, a desire to lead, a love for the people, and a faith-filled heart that must praise God. You are ministering in this role because one thing is clear, the liturgy matters to you.

1. Ephesians 5:18–20.

The sung participation of the faithful should be the music ministry's primary goal.

What Is Liturgy?

Dictionaries will tell you, in one way or another, that *liturgy* is a collection of rites used in public worship. And that is true. But there is much more to liturgy than that. The word *liturgy* comes from a Greek word meaning "public work" or "work of the people." That hits nearer the mark: liturgy is a special kind of work in which the divine and human come together; we do something, and, more importantly, God does something. Liturgy is not a thing; liturgy is an *event*. So let's ask a different question: What does liturgy *do*?

Liturgy gathers us in the presence of God. In speaking of the Eucharist, the second-century *Didache* emphasizes gathering: "Even as this broken bread was scattered over the hills, and was gathered together and became one, so let Your Church be gathered together from the ends of the earth into Your kingdom."[2] Here the Eucharistic bread, formed from many grains of wheat, is an image of what we are to be: disparate individuals who become something new— a worshiping assembly. In the Bible, the gathering of God's people is a sign of the in-breaking of the kingdom of God. Think of Isaiah's vision of a great banquet on a mountaintop.[3] Think of Jesus feeding the multitudes[4] or of the disciples gathered in prayer in the upper room on the first

2. *The Didache: The Lord's Teaching Through the Twelve Apostles to the Nations*, 9. http://www.newadvent.org/fathers/0714.htm; accessed August 28, 2019.

3. See Isaiah 25:6–9.

4. See Matthew 14:13–21, Mark 6:30-44, Luke 9:10–17, and John 6:1–15.

Pentecost.[5] When God gathers his people together, something happens. The same is true of the liturgy. Before a word has been spoken or a note sung, the liturgy is already a sign of the kingdom of God because it gathers us together.

Liturgy helps form us into a community. The act of being together at table, of sharing the Word of God, of being one voice in our sung and spoken prayers, has an impact on us. It is through this shared action in the liturgy that we learn to recognize ourselves as a family of believers, the Body of Christ, and to be united in our action outside of the church as well. We join in the liturgy because we are a community, but the reverse is also true: without the liturgy, we are not a community at all.

Liturgy is both common and cosmic. The liturgy takes the most ordinary things—our bodies and voices, light and darkness, water and fire, bread, wine, and oil, time itself—and, through the action of the Holy Spirit, transforms all of these into God's very presence. The liturgy teaches us to see that the entire universe is marked with the presence of Christ. The "seeds" of God are everywhere in the world. The stuff of our holiness is not far away, remote, or arcane. The common is holy.

Christian liturgy is always about the paschal mystery. At the heart of all Christian prayer is the paschal mystery—that is, the life, death, and resurrection of Christ. Whether our prayer is the Mass, the Liturgy of the Hours, a saint's day, a sacrament—whether it is Advent or Christmas Time, Lent, Triduum, or Easter Time—the liturgy is always about the paschal mystery. Why is the paschal mystery so important? Because, in the words of St. Paul, "if Christ has not been raised, your faith is vain; you are still in your sins."[6] The paschal mystery is the fulcrum of history and the dynamic reality which gives meaning to our lives and enlivens our worship. We gather for liturgy in order to be plunged, again and again, into the paschal mystery.

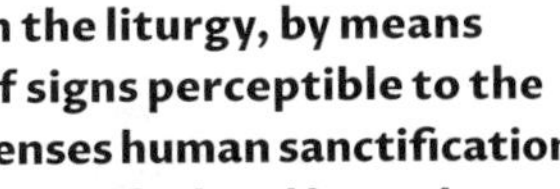

In the liturgy, by means of signs perceptible to the senses human sanctification is signified and brought about in ways proper to these signs.

—*Sacrosanctum concilium*, 7

In the liturgy, we meet Christ. We know that Christ is always close to those who believe: Jesus said, "whoever loves me will keep my word, and my Father will love him, and we will come to him and make our dwelling with him."[7] But in the celebration of the Eucharist, Christ is present to us in a special way. In fact, the Church highlights *four* presences of Christ at Mass. Christ is present in the community gathered for prayer; Christ comes to us in each other. Christ is present in the priest, who acts *in persona Christi*, in the person of Christ, in the Mass. Christ is present in the word proclaimed: "When the Sacred Scriptures are read in the Church, God himself speaks to his people,

5. See Acts of the Apostles 2:1–11.
6. I Corinthians 15:17.
7. John 14:23.

and Christ, present in his word, proclaims the Gospel."[8] And in a unique way, Christ is present in the consecrated bread and wine, his true Body and Blood, shared with us in the Eucharist. Through our participation in this mystery, we meet Christ in many ways and we become what we receive: the Body of Christ.[9]

Liturgy is the worship of the Church. The liturgy is not free-form. As the official prayer of the universal Church, it is governed by universal norms. Most of the texts we hear at Mass—with some significant exceptions, like the homily and the universal prayer—are written down and are the same the world over. Not only the words of liturgy, but most of the actions are the same everywhere: standing, sitting, and kneeling. The liturgical books include many rubrics (from the Latin word for "red," because these instructions are sometimes printed in red ink), which give instructions for how and where each part of the liturgy happens. All of this should remind us that the liturgy does not belong to any one person, priest, or parish. The liturgy is the Church's prayer. But, that does not mean that it is not *our* prayer too. In the words of the Second Vatican Council, the liturgy is "the outstanding means whereby the faithful may express in their lives and manifest to others the mystery of Christ and the real nature of the true Church."[10] Liturgy is our means of expression with Christ and about Christ. In other words, liturgy is the language we speak as Catholics.

The preeminent manifestation of the Church is present in the full, active participation of all God's holy people in these liturgical celebrations, especially in the same eucharist.

—*Sacrosanctum concilium*, 41

The liturgy is richly varied. While the liturgy is carefully governed by liturgical books, it is never monotone. It is constantly changing, with different readings for every day of the year, and different prayers for most days. Through the liturgical year, the Church invites us to meditate on different aspects of the mystery of Christ, from his conception to his second coming. The liturgy is colorful!

The Eucharist is the most important of the Church's liturgies, but it is not our only liturgy. The liturgies of the Church also include rites like those in the *Rite of Christian Initiation of Adults* and the *Order of Christian Funerals*. They include celebrations of the other sacraments, from baptism, confirmation, and Eucharist to anointing and penance, matrimony, and holy orders. In addition, the Liturgy of the Hours, prayed daily by deacons, priests, bishops,

8. *General Instruction of the Roman Missal* (GIRM), 29.

9. See *Sacrosanctum concilium* (SC), 7. This document is also commonly referred to by its English title, the *Constitution on the Sacred Liturgy*. The paragraphs in Church documents are numbered sequentially. The references throughout this resource refer to the corresponding paragraph numbers in the quoted document. Universal Church documents are usually issued first in Latin. Throughout this resource, the Latin titles of these documents have been used. The English titles refer to those documents that are issued by the United States Conference of Catholic Bishops.

10. SC, 2.5.

religious, and many laypeople, is part of the Church's liturgy, sanctifying the hours of each day with prayer to God.

Liturgy is different from devotion. The Church has a rich and wonderful array of devotional prayer—novenas, chaplets, the Rosary, the Way of the Cross, among others—which can enrich our prayer and bring us closer to Christ and to his Mother. The Rosary has a special place in the life of the Church, for, in the words of St. John Paul II, it "serves as an excellent introduction and a faithful echo of the Liturgy, enabling people to participate fully and interiorly in it and to reap its fruits in their daily lives."[11] These devotions can enrich, but must never replace, our participation in the liturgy.

Music is an expression of our faith and it forms our faith.

Liturgy both reflects and shapes our faith. A medieval scholar expressed this in a phrase that has become famous: *lex orandi, lex credendi*, which can loosely be translated as "the law of prayer shapes the law of belief." In other words, the way we pray informs our theology. If you look at the footnotes in the documents of the Second Vatican Council, and in the *Catechism of the Catholic Church*, you'll notice that the sources cited for key teachings not only include the Bible and teachings of popes and councils, but prayers from the Mass. Liturgy is a school of prayer and a school of faith, teaching us to believe with the Church.

The medieval adage is often extended to read *lex orandi, lex credendi, lex vivendi*—"law of life." The way we pray shapes what we believe—and the way we live our lives. Authentic worship and faith lead to discipleship. If it doesn't, it means the transforming power of the liturgy is not really reaching us. As Pope Benedict XVI has written, "A Eucharist which does not pass over into the concrete practice of love is intrinsically fragmented."[12]

Liturgy really matters. *Sacrosanctum concilium* of the Second Vatican Council had this to say about liturgy: "the liturgy is the summit toward which the activity of the Church is directed; at the same time it is the font from which all the Church's power flows."[13] Liturgy is both source and summit, culmination and starting- place. All the preaching and evangelizing the Church does is meant to draw people to Christ in the celebration of the Eucharist. At the same time,

11. *Rosarium Virgins Mariae*, 4.
12. *Deus caritas est*, 14.
13. SC, 10.

though, the Eucharist is not a stopping place. Liturgy is the fountain from which we draw strength to do Christ's work in the world. Liturgy gathers us; liturgy also sends us forth. And if liturgy fails to do that, there is a problem. "We cannot delude ourselves," wrote St. John Paul II, "by our mutual love and, in particular, by our concern for those in need we will be recognized as true followers of Christ. . . . This will be the criterion by which the authenticity of our Eucharistic celebrations is judged."[14]

The Privilege to Serve

Liturgical ministers have the wonderful privilege of helping others participate in this transforming reality we call the Church's liturgy. Whether we are proclaiming a Scripture reading, taking up the collection, distributing Communion, carrying a candle, or preparing the liturgical environment, our goal is the same: to help others find in the liturgy what we have found—a community of believers, a school of holiness, a place of encounter with Jesus Christ. When we go to Mass, we never come out the same, because liturgy is meant to change us. No wonder, then, that the Church puts such emphasis on participation in the liturgy. If we participate fully, consciously, and actively in the liturgy, we cannot fail to be transformed and do our part to transform the world we live in. As liturgical ministers we are called to do just that, and to help others do the same.

Questions for Reflection and Discussion

1. How is praying with a community different than praying on your own? Why do you think Jesus calls us to pray in both ways?
2. What liturgies of the Church do you participate in on a regular basis?
3. Where and when do you feel closest to Christ?
4. Think about the ways Christ is present in the liturgy and in the world. Think of a time when you have felt Christ's presence in these places.
5. Do you find that participating in the liturgy affects your life outside of the liturgy?

14. *Mane nobiscum Domine*, 28.

Chapter Two

The Meaning and History of Your Ministry

Sing praise to the LORD with the lyre,
with the lyre and melodious song.

—Psalm 98:5

Liturgical prayer is worship by a particular group that miraculously shares in the worship of the whole Church. The Catholic Church oversees her liturgical prayer with an impressive array of guidelines for the entire assembly and the ministers who serve her. Whenever the faithful gather for Mass, they join the prayer of the worldwide Church in her great act of thanksgiving.

This is true even of the smallest groups. While on a missionary journey to Philippi, Paul and Silas were imprisoned after performing an exorcism. Locked up in the innermost cell with their feet secured to a stake, Paul and Silas prayed and sang hymns to God at midnight, as other prisoners listened.[1] Unable to worship with bread and wine, they used the elements at their disposal—the psalms and hymns they had committed to memory after much experience with liturgical prayer.

Every member of the assembly has a role to play. Whenever you come to worship, even when you are not serving as a minister of music, you serve as a minister of the assembly, as one who prays and sings. "Christ is really present in the very liturgical assembly gathered in his name."[2] He is present when the Church prays and sings.[3] Each of us has a part to play at Mass. Together we form the Body of Christ.

Christ is really present in the very liturgical assembly gathered in his name.

—*General Instruction of the Roman Missal*, 27

Our role at Mass takes on many forms. Before the liturgy we greet others near the door of the church. We join in the singing to give praise to God. We listen attentively to the Scriptures as they are proclaimed. We observe the postures and gestures together. We share holy Communion together.

We are silent together, to call to mind our sins, to collect our thoughts for prayer, to reflect on the readings and the homily, and to thank God for the gift of the Eucharist. During the Eucharistic Prayer, each member of the assembly is to pray along with the priest.

1. See Acts of the Apostles 16:25.
2. GIRM, 27.
3. See SC, 7.

> The meaning of this Prayer is that the whole congregation of the faithful joins with Christ in confessing the great deeds of God and in the offering of Sacrifice. The Eucharistic Prayer requires that everybody listens to it with reverence and in silence.[4]

When the Mass is over, we leave together. We go out together into the world and carry the message of Christ. In doing so, the word may take root in the hearts of others, just as it has in ours.

Every member of the assembly shares these responsibilities. You have them whenever you exercise your ministry of music, and you have them when you do not.

As a minister of music, you help the entire assembly fulfill its role. You lead the singing. You manage the length of the silences. You model participation by your prayer and attention. You maintain a faith that leads to song in the freedoms of grace or the prisons of sin. No matter the circumstances of your life, you express your faith in music.

The Power of Music

"A liturgical service takes on a nobler aspect when the rites are celebrated with singing, the sacred ministers take their parts in them, and the faithful actively participate."[5] These words from *Sacrosanctum concilium*, the document from the Second Vatican Council that set forth the principles for the renewal of the liturgy mandated by the council, remind us of the important role of the music and music ministers in our worship.

God has bestowed upon his people the gift of song. God dwells within each human person, in the place where music takes its source. Indeed, God, the giver of song, is present whenever his people sing his praises.

—Sing to the Lord: Music in Divine Worship, 1*

Music enriches society. We educate children in the fundamentals of music, so that they will more deeply appreciate what they will instinctively enjoy. Recorded music fills the air around us in shops, cars, homes, and smart phones. Live music is available in many venues—children's recitals, professional concerts, parades, and civic events.

But live music is inconvenient. To enjoy it, most people have to leave home and seek it out. Consequently, the place most people experience live music week in and week out is at church. They hear it and sing it because of you.

Music has powers to channel and express our emotions and beliefs. When it is well composed and well performed, it has a transcendental quality. Good

4. GIRM, 78.

5. SC, 113.

* Referencing 1 Corinthians 3:16–17: "Do you not know that you are the temple of God, and that the Spirit of God dwells in you? If anyone destroys God's temple, God will destroy that person; for the temple of God, which you are, is holy."

music generally follows good compositional conventions. That is, it observes certain structures that make the music work. Good musicians spend hours of time practicing the music, partly to maneuver its physical demands, but more to conquer its emotional meaning. When music is well rehearsed, its message better penetrates the listener.

Each piece of music has an inner heart, just as each poem has a central message, every novel has an overarching theme, and every building has a functional purpose. Whenever we sing or play a piece of music, we reach for its inner heart. If the music is secular, the piece resonates with what it is to be human. When the music is sacred, we realize that what is human exists because of what is divine. When we go to the heart of sacred music, we enter the heart of God.

Within the liturgy, then, music fulfills several needs. When words are to be sung, music enhances the text. Whenever we speak, we raise and lower our voice to indicate what we mean. We form questions with inflections. We lower the volume to suggest intimacy. We raise the volume to gain attention. We stretch words that are important. We swallow words we would rather not say. In music, we stylize the vocal demands of a text. We express the words in ways they cannot express by themselves when they appear on a page and in ways we cannot express when we merely speak.

This common, sung expression of faith within liturgical celebrations strengthens our faith when it grows weak and draws us into the divinely inspired voice of the Church at prayer.

—*Sing to the Lord: Music in Divine Worship*, 5

Music involves people. One of the functions of the entrance chant (or song) is to foster the unity of those who have been gathered.[6] Similarly, at Communion time the song or chant is "to express the spiritual union of the communicants by means of the unity of their voices, to show gladness of heart, and to bring out more clearly the 'communitarian' character of the procession to receive the Eucharist."[7] The Sanctus summons us to sing not just together as an assembly but together with the choirs of angels. Music involves people. It also involves angels, instruments, and the resonance of all God's creation.

Music sets a mood. When instruments play, they evoke the grandeur of a march, the quietude of prayer, the whimsy of spiritual joy, and the gravity of loss. Even without singing or hearing a word, people can be moved by the music at church.

Music creates beauty. It delights the ear and intrigues the mind. It warms the heart and taps the toe. Even when it is completely outside of us, it works its way inside of us. It opens us up to the wonders of God's creation—to the woods, metals, hairs, and hides that make up instruments; to the human vocal

6. See GIRM, 47.
7. GIRM, 86.

Music creates beauty, delights the mind, and gives dignity to ritual prayer.

cords that sing; to the inventive minds that compose music; to the willing hearts that play and sing it. God has created a world that has the potential for music, and God has enabled people to perform and appreciate it. In all of this we encounter the beauty of form and structure, detail, and design. We encounter it live, from human beings sharing their skill, at work with their art, communicating with the composer, communicating with the listener, and communicating with the God who made them all. Whenever we encounter beauty, we encounter an attribute of God.

A world without music would not be lovely. In the violent vision of a tumultuous chapter in the Book of Revelation, an angel prophesies the woes that will befall the sinful city of Babylon. It includes this curse:

> No melodies of harpists and musicians,
> flutists and trumpeters,
> will ever be heard in you again.[8]

Music is a sign of civilization, an endowment for society, and a doorway into the presence of God.

This is music, and it serves an essential part of our common worship. Music is not just something *in* the liturgy; it is *of* the liturgy. It belongs there. It expresses the thanksgiving we offer God, and it reveals the wondrous mystery of God's creative love.

Since the close of the Second Vatican Council in 1965, the Church has witnessed an explosion of ministries that involve music and add to the solemnity of the liturgy. Within Mass people may exercise music ministry in different

8. Revelation 18:22abc.

ways. Someone may play the organ. Others may play piano, guitars, marimba, or other accompaniment instruments. Someone may play a solo instrument to help the assembly sing the melody or to embellish it with a descant. Some people will sing in the choir. Someone directs it. A cantor may sing solo verses. A song leader will cue the assembly when to sing. A psalmist will chant the verses of the responsorial psalm. There are even people who assist behind the scenes with the sound equipment and the preparation of worship aids.

People of all ages, backgrounds, and levels of talent serve in music ministry. Some are professionally trained and have lots of experience while others have little training and limited experience. Some music ministers get paid for their work while many more are volunteers who offer their time and talent. Most parishes have a music director who pulls all the various pieces together and shapes the overall vision for music ministry. The ways in which the music ministry is structured in parishes is quite varied. What is common, however, is that all of the people who serve the music ministry offer their God-given talents to build up the Body of Christ and enhance the communal worship of the Church.

Through grace, the liturgical assembly partakes in the life of the Blessed Trinity, which is itself a communion of love . . . . The Church urges all members of the liturgical assembly to receive this divine gift and to participate fully "depending on their orders [and] their role in the liturgical services."

—*Sing to the Lord: Music in Divine Worship*, 10*

There are many ways to engage in the ministry of music because God has endowed believers with a variety of gifts. When these gifts are put to the service of the Church, they enliven worship with music, faith, and commitment. The Church depends on these gifts for the reception and expression of our faith.

St. Paul asked the Corinthians to use the gifts they had received. Not to use them was like abandoning musical instruments or like fashioning instruments that did not work right.

> If inanimate things that produce sound, such as flute or harp, do not give out the tones distinctly, how will what is being played on flute or harp be recognized?[9]

Music is a gift, and its nature is to be shared. Musicians have a responsibility to share their gift. God gives gifts for the benefit of the entire community. "To each individual the manifestation of the Spirit is given for some benefit."[10] When you share your gift, you proclaim the goodness of God, and the community praises God for the gift you have received.

9. 1 Corinthians 14:7.
10. 1 Corinthians 12:7.
* Quoting SC, 26.

Your voice is your own gift that adds to the new and unified sound of your choir.

The exercise of music takes understanding and expression. After learning the music, a musician expresses it. In liturgical music, learning is a spiritual exercise because the music has something to say about God and the way we worship. Expressing liturgical music is an act of faith. It succeeds when it pulls sincerity from the quiet of the heart into audible melody and rhythm.

As a musician, you may exercise your gift as an accompanist, instrumentalist, singer, or director. If you serve as an accompanist, you lead and accompany. You give introductions. You set the pace of the music. You determine how long the silence is between verses. But you also accompany. You adjust the volume of your instrument to the sound of those who are singing. You let their voice dominate, while you support and react to how they sing. The accompanist takes a confident lead but also takes a humble place behind the voices who sing the words we all address to God.

If you play an instrumental solo, you shape the sound that people hear. You break the silence with your music. You inspire people to be of one heart as they listen. Yet you remember that you are a liturgical musician and not a performer. Your music serves the liturgy. It should make people thankful to God, not to you.

If you sing in the choir, you lend your voice to the overall effect. You may think your voice does not add much in the midst of so many other singers, but it does. Your choir depends on you. You bring the gift of your voice, and it blends with others to form a different voice, a common voice. Each individual voice is like a spice in the sauce. If the salt, pepper, oregano, or garlic is missing, it just won't taste the same. When you sing in a choir, you give up the individual sound of your voice in order to form a new sound. You sacrifice yourself for the sake of the whole. The whole is made more glorious by the gift you give.

If you direct the choir, you create the moment of music. That means you create the moment of faith. As you call the choir into action, you invite them into an act of evangelization. They proclaim the marvels that God has done—indeed, the marvels that God is doing right now as they sing. As the director you oversee the rehearsals, the choice of the music, and the participation of the choir at worship. The choir and the rest of the assembly depend on your leadership in prayer and your leadership in music. Throughout the service you can model prayerful attentiveness to the liturgy. Throughout your life you model a spirit of service.

As a music minister, you will strive to be a model of the Christian life inside and outside the church building. At practice and performance, at home and at school, at work and at play, you will be a model for other Christians. You will be aware of the gifts God has given you. You will want to share them with others. You will recognize these gifts throughout the community. You will encourage others to release the gifts of the Holy Spirit within them. God has given you a gift. You are an instrument in God's hands. Play and sing.

Baptismal Ministry

Sing to the Lord: Music in Divine Worship, a document of the United States bishops, states the importance of the role of music ministers:

> Choir members, like all liturgical ministers, should exercise their ministry with evident faith and should participate in the entire liturgical celebration, recognizing that they are servants of the Liturgy and members of the gathered assembly.[11]

Even though *Sing to the Lord* singles out choir members specifically, it also applies to all those involved in music ministry who exercise their ministry by virtue of their baptism.

Baptism is the foundation of all ministry in the Church. Before you are a music minister, you are a baptized member of the Body of Christ, with all the attendant blessings and duties.

Baptism helps you personally: it cleanses you from sin and incorporates you into the Body of Christ. Baptism also gives you responsibilities toward others: it assigns you a place among the faithful who worship at the Eucharist and who serve their neighbor in the name of Christ. Baptism summons you to worship and service.

As a believer, your role at Mass is so important that, together with others at church, you are called a priestly people. All the faithful join with the celebrant to give thanks to God and offer the sacrifice. In doing this, they also learn to offer themselves completely to God.[12] The law about going to Mass on

11. *Sing to the Lord: Music in Divine Worship* (STL), 32.

12. See GIRM, 95.

Sunday is not to "attend" Mass but to "participate" at Mass.[13] All the baptized have something to do there. It is not just the priest who offers—all the priestly people offer themselves, offer the sacrifice, and share the communion.

We become a priestly people at baptism. During the ceremony, a child is anointed on the crown of the head with chrism, while the priest or deacon says:

> Almighty God, the Father of our Lord Jesus Christ,
> has freed you from sin,
> given you new birth by water and the Holy Spirit,
> and joined you to his people.
> He now anoints you with the Chrism of salvation,
> so that you may remain members of Christ,
> Priest, Prophet and King,
> unto eternal life.[14]

Christians are anointed into the ministry of Christ as leaders. Our participation at Mass is priestly: "The faithful indeed, by virtue of their royal priesthood, share in the offering of the Eucharist."[15] They do so in other ways as well: "They exercise that priesthood, too, by the reception of the sacraments, by prayer and thanksgiving, by the witness of a holy life, self-denial and active charity."[16]

Baptism seals us for worship and marks us as children of God. Because it is received only once, baptism imparts a special character for this purpose: "Incorporated into the Church by Baptism, the faithful are appointed by their baptismal character to christian religious worship."[17]

Thus the three Sacraments of Christian Initiation so work together that they bring to full stature the Christian faithful, who exercise in the Church and in the world the mission of the entire Christian people.

—*Christian Initiation*, "General Introduction," 2

The *Catechism of the Catholic Church* reiterates this baptismal theology:

> Incorporated into the Church by Baptism, the faithful have received the sacramental character that consecrates them for religious worship. The baptismal seal enables and commits Christians to serve God by a vital participation in the holy liturgy of the Church and to exercise their baptismal priesthood the witness of holy lives and practical charity.[18]

13. See *Code of Canon Law*, 1247.
14. *Order of Baptism of Children* (OBC), 62.
15. *Lumen gentium* (LG), 10.
16. LG, 11.
17. LG, 11.
18. *Catechism of the Catholic Church*, 1273; referencing LG, 11 and 10.

Marked for worship, the faithful are also set apart for service. At confirmation, the baptized receive the fullness of the Holy Spirit. The Spirit comes with spiritual gifts, intending us to use them.

> The gift of the Holy Spirit . . . will be a spiritual seal, by which you will be conformed to Christ and will be made more fully members of his Church. For Christ himself, anointed by the Holy Spirit in the baptism he received from John, was sent forth for the work of his ministry, to pour out on the earth the fire of the same Spirit.[19]

This service takes many forms, as the Holy Spirit's gifts do. We care for the sick; we educate the youth; we bring relief to the traumatized; we advocate for life. The service we offer is not a merely humanitarian effort. It serves the mission of the Church. It proclaims the reign of God. The command of Jesus to love our neighbor motivates us to service. When we act on what we believe with the intention to do God's will, our deeds proclaim to others the Good News of salvation.

The baptized proclaim the Gospel in all circumstances: "Reborn as sons and daughters of God, they must profess publicly the faith they have received from God through the church."[20] But they do this in a special way at the Mass. "Both in the offering [sacrifice] and in holy Communion, in their separate ways, though not indiscriminately, all have their own part to play in the liturgical action."[21]

So that the holy people may sing with one voice, the music must be within its members' capability.

—*Sing to the Lord: Music in Divine Worship*, 27

Besides participating at Mass the faithful have other responsibilities as well. They should develop a religious sense, an inner piety. They should show charity toward the brothers and sisters with whom they share the Eucharist.[22] In short, they show on the outside the faith they hold on the inside.

Believers also show that faith when they perform some specific responsibility at the liturgy.

> The faithful, moreover, should not refuse to serve the People of God in gladness whenever they are asked to perform some particular service or function in the celebration.[23]

Everyone participates at Mass on some level. All sing the songs, make the responses, proclaim the creed, and observe moments of silence. But your task as a music minister is one example of service to the people of God in the celebration of the Mass. As stated emphatically in *Sacrosanctum concilium*,

19. *Order of Confirmation*, 22.
20. LG, 11.
21. LG, 11.
22. See GIRM, 95.
23. GIRM, 97.

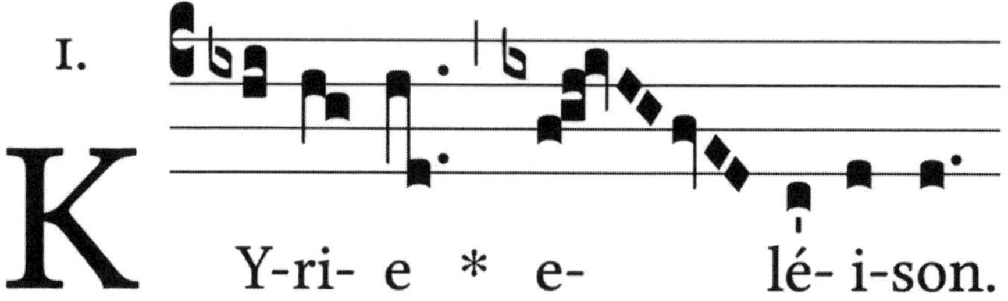

Gregorian chant has pride of place in Roman Catholic liturgy.

"The Church earnestly desires that all the faithful be led to that full, conscious, and active participation in liturgical celebrations."[24]

The Development of Liturgical Music

Liturgical music has become more developed. At first, people probably sang without accompaniment or with an instrument such as the harp. Some of the psalms suggest that parts were sung by a choir or a soloist. For example, in Psalm 24 someone asks, "Who is this king of glory?" And someone responds, "The LORD of hosts; he is the king of glory."[25]

But some of the hymns were sung by everyone together. Many of the New Testament books contain verses that appear to be quotations from popular hymns. For example, "Awake, O sleeper, / and arise from the dead, / and Christ will give you light."[26] Or this one: "If we have died with him / we shall also live with him; / if we persevere / we shall also reign with him. / But if we deny him / he will deny us. / If we are unfaithful / he remains faithful, / for he cannot deny himself."[27] Or this: "Great and wonderful are your works, / Lord God almighty. / Just and true are your ways, / O king of the nations. / Who will not fear you, Lord, / or glorify your name? / For you alone are holy. / All the nations will come / and worship before you, / for your righteous acts have been revealed."[28]

It could have been songs such as these that Paul and Silas sang while chained in a prison cell.

In the early Church, choirs assisted the singing, but everyone sang some part of the liturgy. St. Ambrose of Milan mentions that women alternated with men on some verses. During the Middle Ages, Gregorian chant had become

24. SC, 14.
25. Psalm 24:10.
26. Ephesians 5:14.
27. 2 Timothy 2:11–13.
28. Revelation 15:3–4.

a popular style for singing within at Mass, especially at monasteries. Chant influenced the development of the history of Church music, from the scoring of music to the establishment of a melodic line. The chants were copied out by hand mostly at monasteries, and they were shared from one house of worship to another. Some of these chants were rather difficult and were best mastered by a trained choir. Other chants were simpler and invited singing by the community.

Composers eventually applied the principles of polyphony to vocal music. By dividing choirs into multiple voices or groups of singers, each with its own melodic line, music grew in complexity. Contrasting melodies interacted. The voices pulsed with rhythms. Such music demanded skilled singers, and the work of choirs became detached from that of others. Congregational singing waned as choir music grew more popular.

People distinguished between a low Mass (one without music) and a high Mass (one with music). In the twentieth century the widespread change from the use of Latin to the vernacular affected the music chosen for singing. A long history of great music composed for Latin texts became even more unused, and newer compositions of varying merit were composed to replace them.

It took centuries for the repertoire of Latin Church music to be assembled. It will take a while for good music in English to stabilize.

Other musical instruments may be used in liturgical services, but "the organ is to be accorded pride of place."[29] The organ is one of the oldest musical instruments. In the fourth century St. Jerome knew of one in Jerusalem; it was so loud that it could be heard from the Mount of Olives. Pope St. Vitalian is credited with introducing the organ into the Roman Church in the year 666, to help people sing. Nevertheless, its use was not always welcome. It survived the reforms of the Council of Trent and was popularized for worship in other Christian traditions.

While the organ is to be accorded pride of place, other wind, stringed, or percussion instruments may be admitted into divine worship in the Dioceses of the United States of America, according to longstanding local usage, in so far as these are truly suitable for sacred use, or can be made suitable.

—*General Instruction of the Roman Missal*, 393

In the centuries before the Second Vatican Council, people attending Mass might have heard the organ more than they heard the priest. The priest recited the Eucharistic Prayer in a low voice. In many churches the organist played during this time. Some composers wrote pieces of music called "elevations" to accompany the ritual action. The sound of the organ gave the Roman Mass a distinctive color.

29. GIRM, 393.

After the Second Vatican Council the organ remained a popular instrument for worship. But as new vernacular texts were set to music, they were conceived in a contemporary musical environment that utilized a wider variety of instruments.

St. Cecilia is the patron saint of church musicians.

Representations of St. Cecilia often depict her playing an organ. She is the patroness of church music and church musicians. Little can be verified about the life of Cecilia. She probably lived in third-century Rome and wanted to live as a virgin consecrated to God, but her pagan father set up a wedding. Cecilia sang to God in her heart and prayed for help. She was then able to convince her intended about her vocation. She was later martyred. Her association with Church music probably comes from the report of her singing to God in her heart. There is no evidence she ever played the organ.

Cecilia makes a good patron for musicians regardless of her musical skill. She gave her life to God, her heart to Christ, her efforts to evangelization, and her legacy to future servants of the Church's worship.

Questions for Discussion and Reflection

1. What has been your experience with music?
2. What is your favorite type of music? Why does it inspire you?
3. Have particular songs, hymns, psalms, or chants moved you spiritually?
4. Who are some musicians who have served as models for you? How did they sing? How did they play? How did they live?
5. What can you do to integrate your love of God more fully with your ministerial role?

Chapter Three

Serving as Music Ministers

The musical tradition of the universal Church is a treasure of inestimable value, greater even than that of any other art.

—*Sacrosanctum concilium*, 112

In November 2007, the United States Conference of Catholic Bishops' Committee on Divine Worship approved a new document on music in the liturgy. *Sing to the Lord: Music in Divine Worship* addresses almost every aspect of music ministry we encounter in our daily and weekly lives as those seeking to lead the people of God in song and prayer.[1] The document begins by emphasizing why we sing.[2]

Why *do* we sing?

With many citations from Scripture, like a litany of the songs of God's people through the millennia, the document relates God's instruction to Moses that the Israelites should learn and sing God's words "so that this song may be a witness for me."[3] It tells of the song of the Israelites after crossing the Red Sea,[4] of the song of King David,[5] of the song of Jesus and the apostles before going out to the Mount of Olives,[6] and the song of the saints in glory.[7] "The primordial song of the Liturgy is the canticle of victory over sin and death,"[8] it says. The document reminds us:

> Christ, whose praises we have sung, remains with us and leads us through church doors to the whole world, with its joys and hopes, griefs and anxieties. . . .
>
> Charity, justice, and evangelization are thus the normal consequences of liturgical celebration. Particularly inspired by sung participation, the body of the Word Incarnate goes forth to spread the Gospel with full force and compassion.[9]

---

1. *Sing to the Lord: Music in Divine Worship* replaces the previous documents *Music in Catholic Worship* and *Liturgical Music Today*, and much of the content and teachings of the predecessor documents is brought forward into STL. While STL is not juridically binding and was not submitted to the Holy See for *recognitio* as particular law, it deserves respect and faithful implementation, as guidelines approved by the USCCB. The bishops updated this document in 2012 to bring the language up to date with that of the third edition of *The Roman Missal*.
2. See chapter 1 of STL.
3. STL, 3; quoting Deuteronomy 31:19.
4. See STL, 3.
5. See STL, 3.
6. See STL, 4.
7. See STL, 7.
8. STL, 7.
9. STL, 8–9.

These are powerful words, with a powerful mission behind them: we, the Body of Christ, are to take the song of praise we have sung and bring it out into the world to spread the Gospel. This song is not just for the musicians, not just for the trained, not just for those with beautiful voices—it is the song of the Body of Christ. The "full and active participation by all the people" in this great song "is the aim to be considered before all else, for it is the primary and indispensable source from which the faithful are to derive the true Christian spirit."[10] "Participation in the Sacred Liturgy both expresses and strengthens the faith that is in us."[11] Therefore this participation must be internal, with our full minds and hearts engaged, but it must also be external, reinforcing our inward participation and joining it with others.

Expressing and Strengthening Faith

The first and most obvious role of music ministry is to assist the assembly with finding its own voice, to empower the people with whom you worship how to express their faith with the music they carry within. Music ministers must strive to break down the dynamic of "us" and "them"—the sense that music is something for musicians to do while the rest of the people sit and listen. This view is, sadly, reinforced by our culture's approach to music. Even at sporting events, the national anthem of the United States of America ("The Star-Spangled Banner") is usually begun and sung by some particularly celebrated (or celebrity) soloist. Those attending the game, though some may join in singing, more often simply watch and listen. Expressing ourselves through music, as a group of people singing together with a common voice, is something alien to many in our society.

Through gentle humility, hard work, and much time and patience, you can help people to find the music inside of them. The key thing to remember, before anything else, is that every time you stand up to sing or play, your primary goal and function is to support the song of the assembly. Too many people think they can't sing, when the reality is that singing is a natural human activity. Everyone can sing![12] *Sing to the Lord* says further:

> Singing is one of the primary ways that the assembly of the faithful participates actively in the Liturgy. The people are encouraged "to take part by means of acclamations, responses, psalms, antiphons [and] hymns . . . ." The musical formation of the assembly must be a continuing concern in order to foster full, conscious, and active participation.[13]

---

10. STL, 11; quoting SC, 14.

11. STL, 13.

12. There are, of course, people who are genuinely unable to sing or distinguish pitches, but they are in a very small minority; most of those who think they are "tone deaf" or that they "can't carry a tune" suffer primarily from inexperience or a tragic memory of someone in their past telling them they should keep silent while other more talented or qualified people sing.

13. STL, 26; quoting SC, 30.

If you as a music minister remember and believe this, you will be much more able to communicate it to those with whom and for whom you minister. Over time, you can help them build confidence and find the joy of raising their voices in this fundamental human activity.

In addition to your function of helping the assembly express its faith externally through music, you have a second job: to facilitate music's unique ability to nourish and strengthen the interior participation of those who hear it. Just as the art of singing together as a group has largely faded from our culture, so has the equally crucial art of quiet and meditative stillness, of focused and active quiet and listening. We have screen-in-screen televisions; we watch TV while working on our computers; we are bombarded by sights and sounds almost every moment of the day. Many people (unwisely) have been known to drive the car, eat, and talk or text on the phone all at the same time. *Multitasking* is now part of our way of life. At liturgy, however, our role is more singular and focused; here, we do not multitask.

At liturgy, we are called to be present to, aware of, and focused on the Divine Presence among us. In moments that focus on interior participation, the role of the music minister is different and will be accomplished in other ways: moments of instrumental music before the liturgy or at appropriate times during the liturgy, choral embellishments such as psalm verses in harmony, parts of the service music in alternation with the congregation, or choir anthems to assist in bringing this prayerful focus to the forefront.[14]

The Music Ministers

After its opening section on *why* we sing, *Sing to the Lord* addresses *who* it is that sings—who makes music?

Of special note is the fact that the document speaks first of bishops, priests, and deacons and addresses how important *their* singing is in promoting the prayerful sung participation of the people:

> No other single factor affects the Liturgy as much as the attitude, style, and bearing of the priest celebrant. . . . The importance of the priest's participation in the Liturgy, especially by singing, cannot be over emphasized.[15]

The importance of the priest's participation in the Liturgy, especially by singing, cannot be overemphasized.

—*Sing to the Lord: Music in Divine Worship*, 19

Next, it addresses the gathered assembly, reminding us again that "singing is one of the primary ways that the assembly of the faithful participates

14. It should be noted that, while the various documents refer to music played by the organ or instruments alone, or to selections the choir might sing on its own, there is not a single reference to the cantor singing a "solo" selection of music in any current document.

15. STL, 18–19.

actively in the Liturgy."[16] Only then does it turn its attention to the specific role of the ministers of liturgical music. This is an important distinction. Once again, the document reminds us that ultimately the music in the liturgy is not about the music or the musicians; it is about the prayer of the gathered faithful.

Music Ministers in the Parish

Every parish will have its own style and personality. Some parishes will be more formal and elegant, while others will be more "homey" and intimate. Some liturgies may have only an organist and cantor leading the traditional antiphons, hymnody, and chants of the Church, whereas others may have a full complement of singers and instruments, offering a wide range of musical styles. Some communities may gather people for worship who share basically the same cultural and ethnic background, and others will gather diverse populations with different languages and musical traditions.

Yet music ministers all have one thing in common—the celebration of Christ's paschal mystery encountered in the liturgy. Let's take a look at the different faces of the music ministry you will see in churches everywhere.

The Music Director

The music director in a parish is the person who oversees the entire parish music program. The requirements and work for this position will vary widely from parish to parish. The director in a small community with only one or two liturgies per weekend will have very different responsibilities from the one at the four-thousand-family parish with two adult choirs, three children's choirs, large school and religious education programs, and numerous baptisms, weddings, and funerals.

In some parishes, the music director may hold multiple degrees in organ, conducting, composition, and/or liturgical studies; in others, hard-working and talented amateurs study and learn as much as they can to serve their parishes well. A growing number of parishes, recognizing the impact of quality music ministry on the worship and faith life of their communities, are able to pay a musician a living wage to give full-time professional attention to the work of building and sustaining the musical life of the parish.

The director of music ministries fosters the active participation of the liturgical assembly in singing; coordinates the preparation of music to be sung at various liturgical celebrations; and promotes the ministries of choirs, psalmists, cantors, organists, and all who play instruments that serve the Liturgy.

—*Sing to the Lord: Music in Divine Worship*, 45

In the best situations, the music minister will be someone with formal training and experience in pastoral, liturgical, and musical areas and is

16. STL, 26.

considered to be a fully participating member of the parish staff, with input into all areas of parish life whether specifically music-related or not.

Some parishes have a single director of music ministries who oversees the work of several other music ministers directing different choirs or ensembles, or leading music during specific liturgies. Some must subsist entirely on the work of one or more part-time or even volunteer musicians whose great efforts enable them to manage their parish's music ministry while holding down another full-time job. Some parishes in multicultural communities would perhaps like to have one full-time music director but cannot find a single individual able to lead music and direct choirs in diverse cultural styles and in various languages, and so they divide the job among several individuals.

There are almost as many job descriptions for the music director as there are parishes that depend on hours of diligent work, hard-earned skills, boundless energy, and good hearts to keep their programs going and their people singing.

In most parishes the music director is required to wear a number of different hats and function in varied capacities. The two most frequent jobs usually also held (at least to some degree) by the music director are that of organist/pianist and choir director (see below).

The Organist or Pianist

During almost every liturgy, musical leadership is provided by an individual at whichever keyboard instrument (or instruments) a parish happens to use (normally organ or piano). In many circumstances, it is the same person who serves as music director, although this is not always the case. A skillful keyboardist can use the instrument not just to accompany the liturgical music but also to lead the choir and assembly in their singing, thus enabling the cantor to move away from the microphone so that the voice of the people can be the dominant sound.

The primary role of the organist, other instrumentalists, or instrumental ensemble is to lead and sustain the singing of the assembly and of the choir, cantor, and psalmist, without dominating or overpowering them.

—*Sing to the Lord: Music in Divine Worship*, 41

While a piano or electronic keyboard can certainly be used skillfully to lead a congregation in song (as can other instruments or combinations of instruments), the pipe organ possesses a natural affinity for leading song that is unequalled by any other single instrument. For one thing, its wide variety of stops and registrations enables it to function almost as an instrumental ensemble on its own—sounds reminiscent of flutes, strings, and brass, with a variety of range and tone color that no other single instrument can hope to match. The pipe organ is also genuinely a "wind" instrument, much like the human voice it so ably supports. When a piano key is struck, the sound will immediately begin to diminish or "decay," whereas the organ can sustain

The pipe organ possesses a natural affinity for leading song that is unequalled by any other single instrument.

through the singing as though it had the same breath beneath its sound as the voices singing with it—which, in a very real and literal way, it does. For this reason and many others, the pipe organ is accorded "pride of place"[17] in the liturgies of the Roman Catholic Church.

With rapid strides being made in sound technology, electronic organs and hybrid instruments that combine live pipes with digital sound are now said by some to be almost indistinguishable from a genuine pipe organ (although this question is hotly debated). These electronic or hybrid instruments often are far more affordable for a parish than a pipe organ, although only time will tell if their longevity can even come close to the centuries-long lifespan of a well-maintained pipe organ. The debate among organists about the relative merits of pipe versus electronic organs will no doubt continue, but most seem to agree that if a pipe organ (even a small one) is financially possible, it is usually the better choice, and that if space or finances do not permit the installation of a pipe organ, a well-designed and capably installed electronic or hybrid instrument can be an acceptable and appropriate substitute.

That said, even a less-expensive electronic organ is usually significantly more expensive than a piano (of course, this depends on the piano) or electronic keyboard, so for some parishes the purchase of an organ of any kind may simply not be feasible. Also, much of the music composed since the Second Vatican Council is simply better suited to the piano than to the organ. For this reason, many parishes that take advantage of the best of the Church's repertoire, old and new, try to have both a piano and an organ in their worship

17. GIRM, 393.

space. Organ accompaniments do not always work well played on piano; piano accompaniments do not necessarily translate well to organ. It takes great subtlety and skill to adapt the piano accompaniment of a contemporary-genre piece of music for effective use on an organ and vice versa, and those musicians who cultivate this art find their options greatly increased.

If the organ is a wind instrument, the piano is fundamentally a percussion instrument: each time a key is struck, a hammer strikes the strings with a clearly delineated attack to the note that can project very well through a room. Certainly the many fine pianists who serve in parishes have developed a style of playing that makes optimal use of the piano's percussive nature to support and sustain assembly singing in its own way, as have the composers who create accompaniments best suited to one instrument or the other. The point here is that, despite the identical keyboard layouts of the two instruments, they are exactly that: two different instruments, producing different sounds, requiring different techniques and accompaniment styles, and often suited to different styles of music.

The pipe organ is unique in its ability to create with one instrument the sounds it would normally take many other instruments to produce. Some parishes, particularly when performing music written more recently and in a more contemporary style, are able to have several instruments together leading the sung prayer of the parish. A combination of plucked and bowed strings, woodwinds, brass instruments, and even percussion can together produce great variety of sound and color and give great support to a singing assembly.

In parishes such as these, it is most often the person at the organ or piano who serves as the leader and director, unless the group is fortunate enough to have a separate individual to conduct the group. This requires a different set of skills. This person must be both a leader and an integrated group member, with the ensemble of instruments playing together *as though* they were played by a single individual. The person at the keyboard needs to stay consistently attuned to *everything* that is happening—to the assembly and to those who are singing, as well as to the other instruments.

Those with skill and training on the organ and piano may offer preludes, postludes, and other music chosen from the Church's vast heritage of musical literature. During the parts of the liturgy where specific pacing is necessary, the organist or pianist will often improvise or play small pieces of music to ensure that any given musical moment fits the length of the rite as perfectly as possible. Ultimately, it is the person at the keyboard who has the ability to shape the music within a liturgy and make it "work."

The Choir Director

Choir director is another role often taken by the music director, although parishes with several choirs may have different individuals directing multiple groups. Likewise, often the role of choir director and organist/pianist are combined, with the director leading the choir and instrumentalists from the keyboard for accompanied music and conducting pieces that are sung unaccompanied.

A choir director needs skills that are distinct from those of the accompanist. When directing from the keyboard, the director must be able to convey a sense of the music's tempo and style, both by aural leadership from the instrument and through clear use of body language (head, eye contact, body movement, etc.). Particularly for music that is sung by the choir alone with organ or piano, choirs working with a conductor at the keyboard will generally need very specific instructions regarding entrances, cutoffs, dynamics, articulations, and other style issues, since you will have limited ability to use gesture to communicate these things during the actual performance of the music.

Liturgical musicians are first of all disciples, and only then are they ministers.

—Sing to the Lord: Music in Divine Worship, 49

When you conduct unaccompanied music, or if you are fortunate enough to have a separate accompanist, you have the opportunity to shape the music in a far more immediate and spontaneous manner through use of gesture and body language. A skilled conductor who has devoted much time and study to his or her technique (whether with baton or with hands alone) can, in addition to keeping the group together, communicate subtlety and nuance at a level frequently not possible from the keyboard.

The choir is the director's instrument, and like any instrument, the more time and study one applies to one's ability to play it, the better will be the results.

The Cantor

Cantors often serve in the dual roles of song-leader/animator and psalmist for liturgical celebrations.[18] Although the cantor must be a skilled vocal musician, it is extremely important that he or she also be well trained and formed in the liturgical and pastoral aspects of the cantor's art. When proclaiming the responsorial psalm, the cantor is also a minister of the Word; when leading and supporting the people's song, the cantor is a model for the assembly. The cantor strives to empower the assembly to be comfortable with raising its own collective voice to God in worship.

The Choir or Ensemble

Most parishes will have one or more groups of singers whose song supports and enhances the music for parish liturgies. The names of these groups vary

18. It should be noted that some parishes with the resources to do so are choosing to keep the roles of "cantor" and "psalmist" distinct, by having two individuals serving within a liturgy: one functions solely as a minister of the (sung) word and proclaims the responsorial psalm, and the other leads all other parts of the assembly's sung prayer (see STL, 34–40).

widely from parish to parish. Generally the term *choir* is applied to a larger group of singers, divided into clearly delineated voice parts—soprano, alto, tenor, bass. Choirs are likely to sing music from the Church's musical heritage over the centuries as well as more recent and contemporary selections. The "ensemble," sometimes referred to as the "contemporary choir" or (mostly in years past) the "folk group," is usually a smaller group of singers and instrumentalists specializing in the music composed since the Second Vatican Council. Whether the group is named by age ("adult choir," "youth ensemble," "children's choir"), location of ministry ("chancel choir," "gallery choir"), the time of the liturgy at which its members traditionally minister ("9:00 AM ensemble"), or a more historical ("schola" or "schola cantorum") or creative title ("celebration choir" or "spirit ensemble") the name given to each individual group is far less important than the common role each is called to play in our assembly prayer.[19]

Choirs must be diligently promoted while ensuring that "the whole body of the faithful may be able to contribute that active participation which is rightly theirs."

—Sing to the Lord: Music in Divine Worship, 28*

Like the cantor, ensembles/choirs are considered to be members of the assembly called out from the community, people "who possess the requisite musical skills . . . to enrich the celebration by adding musical elements beyond the capabilities of the congregation alone."[20] They may sing with the assembly, embellish the assembly's song with harmonies and descants, sing in alternation with the assembly, or at some moments in the liturgy sing by themselves—while always remembering that the first concern of all music ministers must be to enable and empower the song of the assembly.

On the surface, this may sound simple. But real life is not always so. When a new song, chant, hymn, response, or acclamation is being learned by the assembly, the temptation to sing a lovely descant or lyrical harmonic line can be great. But your first thought during any part of the liturgy in which the people are invited to sing must be of *their* security and comfort. Only when you are certain the assembly is solid and secure on the melodic lines should you start adding choral embellishments or soaring descants. Adding these elements too soon only underscores people's natural tendency to perceive music as something the "experts" do. Remember, even when the rest of the assembly might forget, you as a music minister are part of the assembly, called to perform a specific role.

19. Please note that the author finds terms like "traditional choir" and "contemporary choir" to be unnecessarily limiting; for example, many "contemporary" choirs will sing "traditional" music, and vice versa.

20. STL, 28.

* Quoting SC, 114.

The Instrumentalists

Aside from the primary keyboard musician, as we mentioned in the section on the organist/pianist, many parish musical groups will have one or more additional players to enhance the musical sound further. These fall into two main groups: rhythm instruments (generally guitar, string or electric bass, and percussion) and obbligato instruments (any single-melody instrument such as violin, flute, trumpet, etc.).

Rhythm instruments will usually work in an ensemble with the keyboard (usually the piano) to create a unified base for the musical accompaniment that is more effective than a piano alone. Bass gives a solid foundation to the sound; guitar fills out the harmonies, and the plucking of its strings adds a percussive effect. In more contemporary music or music from world cultures (particularly those from Latin American or African countries), drums and other percussion instruments can give the music a flavor of authenticity and help hold the rhythmic pulse of the piece together for the assembly.

Obbligato instruments, such as violin, flute, and oboe, can add another layer of musical support and ornamentation. When the assembly is not secure on a piece of music they are invited to sing, these instruments can double the melody and give something else for the assembly's ears to grasp. In choir-only passages or when the people are very solid on their part, obbligato instruments can play their own harmonies and countermelodies. Most publishers offer instrumental parts for some or all of their music; many instrumentalists cultivate the ability to improvise parts on their own.

It should be noted that normally the additional rhythm instruments will combine with the piano alone and the organ much less frequently. Some styles of music (such as music from the African American gospel tradition), however, call for organ to be played together with piano and rhythm instruments. Some music ministers blessed with the presence of two able keyboardists for a single liturgy are learning to make use of the richness of this dual keyboard sound as part of their general music-making.

Hospitality in the Ministry of Music

In a very real way, the ministry of hospitality is a crucial component to the ministry of music. Some of this is implicit in our musical preparation and work. For singing ministers, this means the internalization and familiarity with the text and music being proclaimed, clear enunciation and diction, and carefully placing the focus on the marriage of text and music rather than on you as performer. All efforts to present sung texts clearly and in an easily understood way to the assembly are hallmarks of good and gracious hospitality as well as simple musical skill and quality. Naturally, this same sense of preparation, familiarity, and rehearsal applies just as much to the instrumentalists who lead the music: your support and confident foundation is imperative to strong and joyful singing.

If it is helpful, envision yourself not simply singing or playing a set of words or notes on a page. Think rather of the piece of music as a beloved friend you are introducing to your faith community. Remember the last time you participated in such an introduction of individuals. You step forward only long enough to draw attention to the one being introduced and say something like, "Here is someone we all should meet. . . ." Names are given, and then you step back to allow the new friend's voice to be heard as familiarity grows. It is the same idea with hospitality in music—either introducing a new piece of music, or welcoming into your midst a song or chant already known by all present. Your role is simply to bring the music into the midst of the people with all the clarity and warmth you can, so that it may speak in its own voice to and with the gathered assembly.

Welcome one another, then, as Christ welcomed you, for the glory of God.

—Romans 15:7

Hospitality in music ministry manifests itself in different ways, many of them very subtle. Even for something as small as the announcement of a hymn, there is a world of difference between "Our recessional hymn can be found in the hymnal at number 847" and "As we are sent forth, let us join together in singing, from our hymnal, number 847, 'Alleluia, Sing to Jesus.' Number 847." The first option is brief and not intrusive, to be sure, and it lacks both warmth and the tacit acknowledgment that people will need a little time to gather their books and turn to the correct page; also, the added attention to making certain the people have the opportunity to hear the number well and clearly communicates a genuine desire (and not just lip service) that people have the opportunity to join in song.

The physical mannerisms and body language of music ministers, although difficult to objectively quantify, have a profound effect on how included and invited the gathered assembly feels to take part in singing. The cantor's gesture, for example, is relatively standard. When it is time for the assembly to join in singing, the cantor's arms come up to bring them in. But this simple gesture can have many different shades of expression. Do the cantor's arms simply appear on the first note of the assembly refrain, or do they lift invitingly in the moments before, effectively inviting the assembly not just to sing but also to *breathe* with the cantor? Are the arms and hands stiff and angular like a military salute, or gentle and curved like the invitation to an embrace? Perhaps most important of all (for choirs as well as cantors), do the faces and eyes of the music ministers remain still and unchanging, fixed on the hymnal, or do they raise with the arms, in inviting warmth, making genuine personal contact with the assembly?

To sing is to be vulnerable, and vulnerability is challenging. To lift up one's voice in song, alone or even in a group, can be a very fragile experience. To step up as a cantor or choir member takes even greater courage and vulnerability, and it is a vulnerability from which we dare not hide. The automatic reaction in such a situation is to mentally turn within and close off the connection with those who see our human fragility, those who might hear errors or catch the slightly out of tune note or botched word, to stay guarded and protected. But the essence of hospitality is to embrace that very fragility, to step forward and dare to be human, to meet one another as brothers and sisters in a shared home, and to encourage one another to share in the singing with joy and fearlessness. You are there to underscore and encourage the truth that music is for everyone, and each person's voice is an indispensable part of the song we gather to sing together.

Let the Church always be a place of mercy and hope, where everyone is welcomed and loved and forgiven.

—Pope Francis

"Performance" versus "Prayer"

This is also where the question of "performance" versus "prayer" enters the conversation. Many musicians believe that "performance" is not conducive to ministry. Let's think of this in a different way. The best performers are those who are able to completely disappear into their art—whose skill, knowledge, and physical abilities have been honed so that they are a true and humble vehicle for the music they make. It is the music that is remembered and celebrated. The compliment to the performer is usually around that person's ability to allow the music to express itself through that individual's skill. Can the music minister ask for any more humble or perfect attitude than this? On the other hand, prayer is usually defined as a form of communication or communion with God; can we "pray" in this sense without keeping our own individual selves very aware and conscious?

This could open up a lengthy discussion; however, it might be a good idea to give some serious consideration to what it can mean to "perform." If you believe that the music you make has something to say, or that God has something to say through it (and there's no sense in singing or playing if this is not true), then you must allow yourself truly to perform a Christ-centered ministry of transparence and humility, accepting that you are raw material in the potter's hands, to be shaped according to God's will and not your own.

Selecting Liturgical Music

Although the decision regarding what music will be sung for which liturgies is most often in the domain of the music director, it can help all of us to have an idea of the process behind musical choices. Those who make the musical selections for a parish liturgical program take many variables into account (a few of which are given below, in no particular order):

- What proper texts are suggested in the official chant books or *The Roman Missal* for a given Sunday, solemnity, feast, memorial, or weekday, such as the entrance and Communion song?
- What are the readings of the day, and what music will best evoke the presented scriptural images?
- What is the liturgical season? Should the music be more sparse and unadorned, as for the seasons of Advent or Lent, or should it be grand and celebratory and filled with Alleluias, as would be appropriate for the seasons of Christmas and Easter?[21]
- What is the repertoire of the parish? What songs or chants do the people of this parish sing solidly and with confidence?
- What is the primary language of the gathered assembly? Will there be worshipers present who do not speak or understand the dominant language? If so, how can we best serve them?

Above and beyond all of these considerations must be a deep understanding of the role music is called to play in the liturgy. The very first writings from the Second Vatican Council are very clear about music's role in the liturgy and what it is that makes sacred music *sacred*: it "will be the more holy the more closely it is joined to the liturgical rite."[22] Music in a liturgy is not a series of songs to be "plugged in" at prescribed spots; it forms an integral part of the whole, intimately wedded to the liturgy itself. We do not sing at liturgy; we sing the liturgy. And once again, as we have said several times before, "full and active participation by all the people is the aim to be considered before all else."[23]

The Church is always at prayer in her ministers and her people, and that prayer takes various forms in her life.

—*Sing to the Lord: Music in Divine Worship*, 15

These reasons, more than any others, are why much of the popular Christian devotional music (such as "praise and worship" music) we may hear on the radio, as well as sacred solo pieces of music, do not always find a good home within the liturgy. However beautiful they may be, if they are not integrally tied to the liturgy and the meaning and purpose of the ritual action, and if their performance means that the assembly is denied the opportunity to

21. STL, 110–14 addresses the principle of "progressive solemnity" in choosing music for liturgical celebrations. The more solemn and grand a liturgical celebration, such as during the great festive seasons or particular solemnities, the more festive music and singing will be found in the liturgy. During Advent and Lent, we are called to observe "a certain musical restraint" (STL, 114) that reflects the simplicity of those seasons and does not anticipate the full joy of Christmas and Easter.

22. SC, 112.

23. SC, 14.

participate fully, actively, and consciously, they do not belong in our Church's corporate or public worship.

The documents of the Church, and particularly *Sing to the Lord*, provide criteria for musical selection. These criteria have been referred to as the "three judgments": liturgical judgment, pastoral judgment, and musical judgment. These judgments are to be considered together, in balance, not allowing one to dominate the others or any to be dismissed as irrelevant: three judgments, one evaluation.[24]

The liturgical judgment asks, "Does this piece of music serve the liturgy as it should?"[25] The pastoral judgment asks, "Does this piece of music serve this assembly, at this moment, in this situation?"[26] Finally, the musical judgment asks, "Is this piece of music good? Is it a well-crafted and quality piece of art?"[27] Again, these judgments are not to be seen as three separate principles but as one guiding standard or practice. They are called on to always work in harmony and dialogue with one another in decisions regarding music in the liturgy.

Documents on Music and the Liturgy

Often the best way to get at the "hows" and "whys" of liturgical preparation is to go, quite literally, to the sources. Thus far, this portion of this book has relied heavily on quotes from various liturgical documents for guidance and reference; if you have never read them before, take some time to examine some of the Church's documents regarding liturgical music. The documents provide invaluable insight into the deeper facets of music ministry and portray music's

24. See STL, 126.

25. "Is this composition capable of meeting the structural and textual requirements set forth by the liturgical books for this particular rite? Structural considerations depend on the demands of the rite itself to guide the choice of parts to be sung, taking into account the principle of progressive solemnity (see nos. 110ff. in STL). A certain balance among the various elements of the Liturgy should be sought, so that less important elements do not overshadow more important ones. Textual elements include the ability of a musical setting to support the liturgical text and to convey meaning faithful to the teaching of the Church" (STL, 127–28).

26. "The pastoral judgment takes into consideration the actual community gathered to celebrate in a particular place at a particular time. Does a musical composition promote the sanctification of the members of the liturgical assembly by drawing them closer to the holy mysteries being celebrated? Does it strengthen their formation in faith by opening their hearts to the mystery being celebrated on this occasion or in this season? Is it capable of expressing the faith that God has planted in their hearts and summoned them to celebrate? . . . Other factors—such as the age, culture, language, and education of a given liturgical assembly—must also be considered. Particular musical forms and the choice of individual compositions for congregational participation will often depend on those ways in which a particular group finds it easiest to join their hearts and minds to the liturgical action. Similarly, the musical experience of a given liturgical assembly is to be carefully considered, lest forms of musical expression that are alien to their way of worshiping be introduced precipitously" (STL, 130 and 132).

27. "The musical judgment asks whether this composition has the necessary aesthetic qualities that can bear the weight of the mysteries celebrated in the Liturgy. It asks the question: Is this composition technically, aesthetically, and expressively worthy? This judgment requires musical competence. Only artistically sound music will be effective and endure over time" (STL, 134–35).

role within the liturgy. Some of the key documents you might start with are described below.

Sacrosanctum concilium is remarkable in that (a) it was the first document written from the Second Vatican Council and (b) it devoted one of its seven chapters entirely to the topic of sacred music in the liturgy. This is the core document from which all other postconciliar documents are drawn. Far from being a dry and academic text (though many passages delve into very specific logistical circumstances), this spiritual jewel of liturgical writing should be read by everyone in any liturgical ministry role.

As this title suggests, *the General Instruction of the Roman Missal* is a solid "how-to" manual for all aspects of celebrating the Mass. It addresses the purposes and forms for each part of the Mass; the different roles taken by ministers and faithful; postures for the Mass (sitting, kneeling, or standing); questions of environment, furnishings, vestments, and, of course, music. It is also the first place to look when faced with a question regarding the correct way to accomplish something within the liturgy. The document also clearly explains the "whys" behind the different aspects of how liturgy is celebrated.

Musicam sacram is both the first document written entirely on liturgical music (written following the Second Vatican Council) and the only such document given to us by the Vatican. On the one hand, its promulgation so soon after the Council means that it was written before the revised rite had full opportunity to emerge; on the other hand, it provides a solid foundation for the thought and intention for ritual music as provided by the council.

Sing to the Lord: Music in Divine Worship stands as the "how-to" manual for parish music ministers. It addresses both specific musical issues and wider theological and ideological questions and implications for liturgical music. *Sing to the Lord* expands on the "three judgments" for selecting music for liturgy: the liturgical judgment, the pastoral judgment, and the musical judgment. Spend some time with this document; invite fellow choir members, cantors, and instrumentalists to likewise spend time with it. Gather together as music ministers to discuss and pray around this resource. It is a wonderfully rich piece of pastoral writing that would give any music minister much wonderful material to reflect on.

Beginning to step forward into awareness and familiarity with the Church's documents on music can be a little intimidating at first, but they are filled with treasures of wisdom from which all of us can benefit.

Songs, Hymns, and Chants: A Question of Terminology

Throughout the documents and writings regarding liturgical music, various terms are used to refer to music used at different times in the liturgy. Three terms that become particularly confusing are *song*, *hymn*, and *chant*.

For many of us, **chant** evokes the image and sounds of Gregorian chant, smoothly flowing monodic (single-line melody) music without set rhythmic patterns. The *General Instruction* uses the term *chant*, however, to apply to music throughout the liturgy at many different points, regardless of style or genre: it speaks of the "entrance chant" and the "Communion chant," and it even refers to the responsorial psalm and Gospel acclamation as chants. Most of us have become habituated to refer instead to the "entrance song" or "entrance hymn," for example. The term *chant* feels slightly awkward to us and calls to mind a genre and form of music that the particular piece of ritual music may or may not reflect.

Likewise, the term **hymn** tends to be used as a blanket term for any sacred song. In practical terminology, however, it is somewhat more specific. Most musicians agree that the term *hymn* is reserved for a piece of music in strophic form, with repeated melodic stanzas sung to a different text each time. A Gregorian chant setting of an entrance antiphon interspersed with psalm verses would not be a hymn; nor would a song such as "Eagle's Wings" or "Gift of Finest Wheat."

Song, then, is the third of these three terms. In many ways it is the most generic of the three and has the least clearly definable set of characteristics. For this reason, and due to the pastoral reality that our musical styles and genres differ widely from parish to parish, we will primarily adopt the term *song* throughout this book as a general term for a piece of liturgical music.

Musical Forms

Also playing an important role in the selection of music for liturgy is a consideration of the different musical forms that tend to occur and recur in the liturgy. The different musical parts of the liturgy, in almost any parish, will usually break down into one of the following six structural forms:

Strophic Form

Also known as "hymn" form, this is the form used in most traditional hymnody. In a strophic hymn or song, a melodic stanza is sung several times with a different text each time; there is no refrain and no concrete repetition of text from one verse to the next. (Examples: "Joyful, Joyful, We Adore You"; "Holy God, We Praise Thy Name.")

Verse-Refrain Form

This consists of a series of verses that lead to a consistent refrain after each one. Much contemporary popular music is written in this form, and a great deal of contemporary liturgical music has followed this pattern also, on the theory that assemblies will pick up and even memorize a repeated refrain more quickly than a hymn with a great many words that never repeat. (Examples: "On Eagle's Wings"; "How Great Thou Art.")

Responsorial Form

Although the word *responsorial* is most often used to describe the sung psalm in the liturgy, responsorial singing occurs whenever there is a dialogue between cantor and assembly, wherein the cantor sings a verse and the assembly responds with a consistent refrain. (Examples: see music from any responsorial psalm collection or Gospel acclamation.) Please note that the difference between a piece of music in verse-refrain form and one in responsorial form will very often simply be in the choice of how to sing it. Much contemporary liturgical music was originally conceived to be sung responsorially, with the cantor singing the verses and the assemblies taking their part on the refrains; however, as the music became familiar and well-loved by the people, assemblies have begun to join in and take ownership of the verses also. The only places in the liturgy where responsorial singing is specifically called for are the responsorial psalm and the Gospel acclamation; at other places in the liturgy it becomes the music director and cantor's choice, depending on the song and the facility of the assembly.

Antiphonal Form

In its purest form, antiphonal singing would consist of half of the choir or assembly singing alternately from opposite sides of the room;[28] the term means, literally, "sound-against-sound." Antiphonal singing will generally involve a group in dialogue with another group, rather than our more accustomed exchange of cantor in dialogue with assembly. Antiphonal singing is practiced most often in religious communities that chant the Office as two alternating halves of the assembly.

Litanic Form

Litanies are a variation on responsorial form, used in the liturgy primarily at the penitential act, universal prayer, and Lamb of God. Both the cantor's invocation and the assembly's response are generally shorter than in a typical responsorial piece of music, and the dialogue is more immediate and apparent

28. If you were to look at the architecture of some buildings designed for religious communities or many worship spaces from the Anglican tradition, you would likely see "choir stalls" on either side of the room rather than the choir lofts or integrated music areas we have come to expect.

than in most responsorial singing. (Examples: see any musical settings of the penitential act, universal prayer, or Lamb of God.)

Through-Composed Form

This is the name commonly given to those pieces of music with no set repetitions or refrains; they are seen most often in liturgical settings of the eucharistic acclamations (Sanctus, memorial acclamation, and amen) and sometimes the Gloria (although there are currently many responsorial settings of the Gloria in use). For the setting of a prescribed text that does not lend itself to a highly structured form, a through-composed setting is often the most logical choice. (Examples: Sanctus from *Mass of Creation*). Please note that while not technically a correct use of the term, many musicians will also use the term *through-composed* to describe a piece of music with a set refrain but verses that vary melodically from one to the other.

While these are not the only musical forms we will encounter as music ministers, they are by far the most prevalent; if we are comfortable with each of the above forms, we should have no trouble adapting to slightly different styles or hybrid forms that blend them further. And as we will see as we look at the musical moments of the liturgy itself, these forms can be very helpful in assisting us to perform our ministry well.

A Musical Journey through the Mass

As a Catholic your most important hour each week is Sunday Mass. You gather on the day of the resurrection to express your faith that Jesus is the Son of God and that he died and rose to save us. You express that belief with family, friends, and strangers who gather to do together what they cannot do alone. You form a body. You experience the revelation of God as a community. You form the Body of Christ worshiping together and bringing the Gospel to the entire world.

As a musician you frequently have a leadership role at Mass. But whether you are the musician every week or just once in a while, your participation at Mass each week is crucial for your own spirituality and the integrity of your parish. Your brothers and sisters in Christ need you there.

Let's take a walk through a typical weekend Mass and examine the way music weaves through the fabric of Sunday Mass.

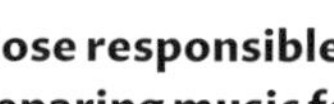

Those responsible for preparing music for the celebration of the Eucharist in accord with the three preceding judgments must have a clear understanding of the structure of the Liturgy.

—*Sing to the Lord: Music in Divine Worship*, 137

Introductory Rites

The Introductory Rites may consist of the following:

- Entrance Procession/Entrance Song
- Sign of the Cross and Greeting
- Penitential Act and Kyrie—*or*—Rite of Blessing and Sprinkling of Water
- Gloria
- Collect

The purpose of the Introductory Rites is to help the assembled people "come together as one,"[29] preparing them for hearing God's Word and celebrating the Eucharist.

The Entrance Song

The liturgy begins with a song whose purpose is fourfold: it is intended to "open the celebration, foster the unity of those who have been gathered, introduce their thoughts to the mystery of the liturgical season or festivity, and accompany the procession of the priest and ministers."[30] The role of the music ministry is to give enough support so that the assembly can sing with strength, without being overpowered.

There is the option of singing the entrance antiphon, or introit. These antiphons are brief refrains with or without chanted psalm verses, which are specified for the start of each Sunday's liturgy.[31] These are most likely to be sung in a responsorial or litanic form, requiring a different leadership approach than a song or hymn sung by the assembly throughout. The proper antiphons assigned to each liturgy are found in Latin chant in the *Graduale romanum*. Easier Latin antiphons that can be used throughout a season are found in the *Graduale simplex*. Texts from either of these two sources can be sung in an English translation; because no official translation exists, the composer is free to use any translation. The entrance and Communion antiphon texts in *The Roman Missal* are often but not always identical to the texts of the *Graduale romanum*. They are intended for reciting at Masses without music, but one is free to use these texts in sung form also.

If the entrance song is in a metered (steadily rhythmic or strophic) style, instrumentalists should set down a clear and steady rhythmic pulse, and vocal musicians (choirs or cantors) should sing clearly but with only as much harmonic embellishment as the assembly can accept without becoming confused or distracted. If a free-rhythm or chanted setting of the antiphon or other song

29. GIRM, 46.

30. GIRM, 47.

31. A specific antiphon is provided in *The Roman Missal* for each day of Advent, Christmas, Lent, and Easter, as well as individual solemnities and feasts of the Lord, ritual and votive Masses, and Holy Thursday. Antiphons are also provided for each Sunday in Ordinary Time. The antiphons for Sundays in Ordinary Time may also be used for any weekday in Ordinary Time.

is chosen, slightly different strategies for empowering the assembly's song will need to be used, although all strategies generally boil down to clarity, warmth of leadership, and time. Through solid instrumental leadership, appropriate microphone use (or non-use), and clear, well-thought-out gesturing by the cantor, your music ministers will be able to empower the assembly to sing well and comfortably, without drawing undue attention to themselves.

Sign of the Cross and Opening Greeting

After the entrance song, the priest makes the sign of the cross and greets the assembly to signify "the presence of the Lord to the assembled community."[32] The assembly sings the response, with choir and cantors joining with the assembly while modeling good sung participation.

Penitential Act and the Kyrie

In the penitential act, the priest invites the gathered faithful to a communal repentance and rejoicing in the infinite mercy of God. After a moment of silence in which those gathered recall their sin, the penitential act is prayed.

There are three options this can take. In the first option, the assembly prays the Confiteor together ("I confess to almighty God . . ."). The second option, the briefest of the three, is a dialogue between priest and people asking for God's mercy, love, and salvation. In each of the first two options, the words of absolution are then spoken by the priest.

In the first and second, after the words of absolution are spoken, the Kyrie is sung or spoken. It consists of a simple threefold litany praying for God's mercy and compassion: Lord, have mercy; Christ, have mercy; Lord, have mercy (*Kyrie eleison, Christe eleison, Kyrie eleison*). Either the vernacular or the Greek may be used.

The third option of the penitential act is slightly different. In this form, the Kyrie is incorporated into the rite itself and forms a slightly longer litany. The assembly is invited to respond after each of three "tropes," expanded texts found in the missal. In this option, the words of absolution follow the Kyrie and complete the rite.

Because of the communal nature of this part of the rite, normally the Kyrie will involve the gathered assembly in some way, often in dialogue with the choir or cantor.

Rite of Blessing and Sprinkling of Water

Particularly during Easter Time, the rite of blessing and sprinkling of water may replace the penitential act and Kyrie. Following the prayer of blessing over the water, the priest sprinkles the gathered faithful with the holy water as a song or antiphon is sung. This song will always be baptismal in nature and

32. GIRM, 50.

can take almost any musical form; it can be sung by the choir alone or by the cantor or choir with the assembly.

GLORIA

The Gloria is "a most ancient and venerable hymn"[33] of praise to God that forms part of the "ordinary" of the Mass[34] and is to be proclaimed during all Sunday liturgies except for those in the penitential seasons of Advent and Lent. The Gloria is also sung on solemnities and feasts. Settings of the Gloria are many and varied; some are in responsorial or song form, and others are through-composed; some are sung by the choir alone, some by everyone gathered together, and some by the choir or cantor in alternation with the assembly.

COLLECT

After a communal invitation to a brief, silent prayer, the collect is prayed by the priest. The words of this prayer draw the attention of the assembly to the mysteries celebrated in a particular Mass. If the priest chants the collect, the people will chant back their response, "Amen."

Liturgy of the Word

The Liturgy of the Word and the Liturgy of the Eucharist are the two primary parts of the Mass and are intimately connected. In the Liturgy of the Word, Christ himself, the Word made flesh, is present in the proclamation of Scripture (both Old and New Testaments). These ancient and holy texts are traditionally proclaimed from the ambo, the table of the Word—as the altar is the table of the Eucharist. This is where God speaks the truth of salvation to the gathered assembly.

The Liturgy of the Word includes the first reading, responsorial psalm, second reading, the Gospel, homily, profession of faith (creed), and the universal prayer or prayer of the faithful.

READINGS

Lectors and readers have the option of chanting the readings, provided the singing serves to bring out the sense and meaning of the words and does not cause them to get lost. In addition, or alternatively, they may chant, "The Word of the Lord" at the conclusion to the readings, with the people responding, "Thanks be to God."[35]

---

33. GIRM, 53.
34. The "ordinary" of the Mass is made up of those texts that do not change but are constant from week to week throughout the liturgy. These include the following: Kyrie (Lord, have mercy), Gloria, the creed (profession of faith), Sanctus (holy, holy, holy), and Agnus Dei (Lamb of God). This is in contrast to the "proper" of the Mass, those prayers and readings that change from week to week throughout the cycles of the liturgical year and that include the responsorial psalm and the entrance and Communion antiphons. In the reformed liturgy it is probably more helpful to distinguish between songs that accompany a rite (such as the Alleluia or acclamation before the Gospel or the Agnus Dei) and songs that form an independent rite themselves as an integral part of the liturgy (such as the Gloria or responsorial psalm).
35. See STL, 153–54.

Responsorial Psalm

The psalm that follows the first reading is an integral part of the Liturgy of the Word and is normally led by the cantor/psalmist from the ambo. While there are some beautiful choral settings of responsorial psalms, it is important to remember that at this point in the liturgy the one(s) proclaiming the psalm is serving as a minister of the Word, not primarily as a minister of music. The beauty of the music in the psalm should always point toward, never distract from, the text being proclaimed.

Normally, a responsorial congregational form will be used, and all efforts possible should be made to enable the people to sing their part with strength and ease. It is also possible to sing a metrical psalm; that is, a strophic metrical version of the assigned psalm text to a metered hymn tune, as a way to enable the congregation to sing the psalm even when no cantor is present.[36] In addition to the "proper" psalm for each week, the lectionary provides several seasonal psalm settings, intended to provide parishes with an alternative for assemblies that find it difficult to learn a new psalm response each week.[37]

Parishes are invited to make use of various options; in fact, the latitude given by the various liturgical documents regarding the responsorial psalm is an indication of the value placed on its being well sung by the assembly.[38]

Although the responsorial psalm is normally taken from the Book of Psalms, as you would conclude by its title, at some points in the year a canticle (scriptural song) such as the Magnificat (Luke 1:46–55) is sung in its place.

The Sequence

A sequence is a poetic, nonbiblical chant sung during the Liturgy of the Word before the Gospel acclamation. Though at one time there were many sequences sung throughout the liturgical year, the Church as we worship today observes them only on four specific instances: The sequence is always to be sung on Easter Sunday (*Victime paschali laudes*) and Pentecost (*Veni Sancte Spiritus*). The remaining two sequences, *Lauda sion* and *Stabat mater*, sung on the Solemnity of the Most Holy Body and Blood of the Lord and the Memorial of Our Lady of Sorrows, are optional.

The choir or cantor may chant the sequence alone, or the congregation may sing it in a metrical setting as a hymn, or a setting that alternates between

36. See STL, 158.

37. "The proper or seasonal Responsorial Psalm from the *Lectionary for Mass*, with the congregation singing the response, is to be preferred to the gradual from the *Graduale Romanum*" (STL, 157; referencing GIRM, 61 and the Lectionary, 20 and 89).

38. "In addition to the proper or seasonal Psalm in the *Lectionary*, the Responsorial Psalm may also be taken from the *Graduale romanum* or the *Graduale simplex*, or it may be an antiphon and psalm from another collection of the psalms and antiphons, including psalms arranged in paraphrase or in metrical form, providing that they have been approved by the United States Conference of Catholic Bishops or the diocesan bishop. Songs or hymns that do not at least paraphrase a psalm may never be used in place of the Responsorial Psalm (See GIRM, 61). If it is not possible for the Psalm to be sung, the response alone may be sung, while the lector reads the intervening verses of the Psalm" (STL, 158–60).

congregation and cantor or choir. Settings for the sequence are many and varied and are available from numerous publishers and are also found in most standard hymnals and worship resources.

Gospel Acclamation

The Gospel acclamation accompanies the procession with the *Book of the Gospels*. In this song of praise the assembly "welcomes and greets the Lord who is about to speak to them in the Gospel."[39] The acclamation, like the psalm, is also intended to be a responsorial piece of music: the cantor or choir intones the response ("alleluia" during most of the year, replaced by other acclamation responses during the Lenten season), after which it is repeated by the assembly. The cantor or choir then sings the Gospel verse specified for that particular Sunday, and the assembly repeats the "alleluia" or Lenten response.

The priest is also a music minister and may chant the presidential prayers as well as the Gospel.

Gospel

Like the readings, the Gospel may be chanted by a priest or deacon, provided he is able to do it clearly and in a way that brings out the true sense of the text. Similarly, he may choose to chant the greeting and conclusion to the Gospel, with the people responding.

Profession of Faith

The creed (Apostles' or Nicene) may be sung or chanted on Sundays and solemnities, but generally this communal profession of faith is recited by all. If it is sung, it is crucial that the people's ability to participate and express their faith be attended to—whether by use of a simple chanted setting, a congregational refrain, or by alternating with the choir or cantor.

Universal Prayer

The universal prayer or prayer of the faithful is the prayer of the baptized in which those gathered pray to God on behalf of the Church, the world, the oppressed, and the local community. When sung, the cantor chants the prayer of petition and invites the assembly (joined by the choir) to join in the response.

39. GIRM, 62.

Liturgy of the Eucharist

During the Liturgy of the Eucharist, the gathered faithful do what the Lord Jesus Christ himself commanded: eat and drink his own Body and Blood. The Liturgy of the Eucharist begins with the preparation of the gifts, continues with the Eucharistic Prayer, and concludes with the Communion Rite (Lord's Prayer, sign of peace, Lamb of God, reception of holy Communion, and prayer after Communion).

Offertory Song

The Liturgy of the Eucharist begins with the preparation of the gifts. Monetary contributions are collected, the altar is prepared, and members of the liturgical assembly customarily bring the gifts of bread and wine to the priest or deacon. This song may take almost any musical form (normally strophic or verse-refrain), although this is also an appropriate moment for a piece of music sung by the choir alone or for instrumental music.

Preface Dialogue

The preface dialogue begins the Eucharistic Prayer. If possible, it is preferred that the priest celebrant chant this dialogue, inviting the assembly to join in singing the responses. In this moment, the music ministry generally functions as members of the assembly, providing specific leadership only as needed to enable the participation of the people. The preface dialogue, especially, is appropriate to have sung because of its expression of collective communion and thanksgiving between and among priest and people.

Eucharistic Prayer and Acclamations

The Eucharistic Prayer is the "center and high point of the entire celebration,"[40] a single prayer needing clear ritual unity from beginning to end. This prayer itself may be sung by the priest celebrant either in part or throughout. While it is most common for the priest celebrant to recite his parts of the prayer after the Sanctus, it is also possible for him to chant these.

During the Eucharistic Prayer, three acclamations (normally well-matched and connected by melodic or stylistic unity) are proclaimed by the assembly:

- The Sanctus (or Holy, Holy, Holy)
- Memorial Acclamation (Mystery of Faith)
- Amen

These are pivotal points within the prayer, normally sung by everyone gathered; they are not normally sung by choir or cantor alone, nor are they normally spoken. It is especially important that these acclamations be

40. GIRM, 78.

comfortable and familiar to the assembly, so that the whole assembly can sing them together. Most parishes will have only a few settings of these acclamations rotating throughout the liturgical year. The choir joins with the assembly in singing these acclamations, modeling for the assembly good sung participation; it is possible for the choir to enhance the assembly's song with descants and supplementary harmonies.

The following "cues" will be helpful to knowing when and what acclamations to sing and play.

- After the preface to the Eucharistic Prayer, the Sanctus is sung. Although there are over eighty prefaces included in *The Roman Missal*, they all follow a similar form. Listen for the concluding verse, which always emphasizes our belief that we join our prayer to that of the angels and saints.
- The memorial acclamation follows the institution narrative and is sung in response to the priest's invitation to "The mystery of faith."
- With the final doxology ("Through him . . ."), the priest affirms and brings to a close the entire Eucharistic Prayer. The assembly's "Amen," sometimes referred to as the great amen, is the people's affirmation and assent to the great mystery they celebrate.[41] Though the doxology and amen may be spoken, it is strongly recommended that at least on all Sundays and solemn occasions these both should be sung.

The Communion Rite

The Lord's Prayer

The Lord's Prayer may be sung. Whether it is the traditional chant version or in a through-composed or more contemporary setting, it is especially important that the people's ability to participate not be impeded in any way. The music ministers should be as transparent as possible, providing only the support and leadership necessary to enable the assembly's singing. It is never appropriate for a soloist or choir to sing the Lord's Prayer alone at any liturgy.

Lamb of God (Agnus Dei)

The Lamb of God (Agnus Dei) is another part of the ordinary of the Mass, also in litanic form. This litany is intended to accompany a specific liturgical action—namely, the breaking of the Eucharistic bread.

Normally the Lamb of God is a threefold litany. It is normally sung with the cantor or choir, alternating with the *assembly*'s response. When a large number of faithful are gathered for Eucharist, and additional extraordinary ministers of holy Communion and vessels are needed, this rite sometimes takes longer than the threefold litany can support. In these cases, the Lamb of God can be extended to cover the ritual action; however, no other

41. "Great Amen" is a more colloquial term; it is not official liturgical terminology.

Christological invocations may be added. The final invocation will always be "Lamb of God" and end with "Grant us peace."[42]

Communion Song

Where assembly participation is concerned, the Communion song presents perhaps the greatest challenge to those in the music ministry. On the one hand, the rites of the Church are clear that this is an ideal moment for song with the entire assembly. On the other hand, the people are walking in procession, receiving holy Communion, consuming the sacred species, returning to their places, and praying. Asking them to sing as well may be asking a lot. The *General Instruction* makes provision for a choir-only piece of music during the Communion Rite, but many parishes are finding that, over time, pieces of music with clear and easily sung refrains are able to be memorized by the assembly and sung without book in hand while people are still moving in procession.[43]

Song of Praise

Following holy Communion, after a few moments of silent prayer, the entire assembly may sing a song of praise.

Prayer after Communion

The prayer after Communion concludes the Communion Rite. Like the collect, it may be chanted by the presiding priest; if the priest chants the collect, the people will chant back their response, "Amen."

Concluding Rites

Following the prayer after Communion, any necessary announcements are made, the final blessing is given, and the assembly is dismissed, transformed by the Word they have heard and the Eucharist they have received.

The Final Greeting, Blessing, and Dismissal

The priest may chant the final greeting and blessing, whether in a simple form or as the more solemn threefold blessing. During the octave of Easter and on Pentecost, the singing of the solemn dismissal with the added alleluia is encouraged.

Closing Song

In the dioceses of the United States of America it has become customary to sing a closing song. This custom is acknowledged in *Sing to the Lord*, which also specifies that such a song is not required and suggests that if a congregational song after Communion was sung, instrumental music might be more appropriate here. If a congregational song is used, generally the text will

42. See STL, 188.
43. See GIRM, 89.

reflect themes of praise, thanksgiving, and the sending forth of God's people to be and serve the Body of Christ in the world.[44]

Music and Other Sacramental Celebrations

In addition to Sunday Mass, music naturally plays a role in all of the special celebrations throughout the liturgical year, including holydays of obligation, the Liturgy of the Hours, orders of blessing, infant baptisms, confirmation, first holy Communion, reconciliation, and Christian initiation to name a few. Ample resources are available to assist musicians in preparing for these rites. The role of music in the Sunday liturgy should be used as your guiding principles for preparing music at these other rites as well. What follows will help you with some specific celebrations.

Sacred Paschal Triduum

Preparing for and executing the various musical pieces of the great Paschal Triduum is perhaps the greatest challenge a music minister faces all year—a liturgy so great it requires three days to complete it!

The sheer volume of music, with little opportunity for repetition, is alone sufficient to make the Triduum a daunting experience. The logistics of preparing and coordinating with other ministers also requires a good deal of attention and alertness. It is crucial that music ministers be included in rehearsals for the various elements of the Triduum to avoid any surprises or missed cues.

One of the first concerns will be the question of who the music ministers at the different Triduum liturgies will be. In parishes with more than one choir or ensemble, the temptation will be great to parcel them out to different groups (who may possess different repertoires and musical styles or even different directors). While this may seem like the expedient option, care must be taken to keep continuity from day to day, making it aurally clear that these three days constitute a single liturgical moment in the life of the parish. Especially if these different musical groups involve different directors, it is imperative that preparations for these liturgies involve all those who will be responsible for directing the various parts, so that each individual knows what the others are doing. Common repertoire, common acclamations, and a common vision go a long way toward creating the unity of purpose necessary to shape this pivotal celebration.

If your parish has the resources, the ideal approach would be to consider developing a "special event" choir, a group that may be a subset of various ensembles who would be willing to lead the music. While it involves a high level of commitment on the part of participants, a group like this can—by its

44. See STL, 199.

very makeup and presence—provide the aural "glue" to connect Holy Thursday, Good Friday, and the great Easter Vigil.

Confirmation and First Eucharist

The sacraments of initiation into the Christian community are special and joyous occasions for any parish, and as with any liturgical celebration, music plays a significant role. These liturgies, whether they occur within Sunday Mass or at a special celebration, are most effectively served when the music chosen is taken primarily from the parish's regularly established repertoire. Although some parishes may choose to have these liturgies ministered by a teenaged or children's choir, remember that these are not primarily "children's" celebrations—they are part of the life of the entire parish community and should be treated as such. Naturally, all of the norms and characteristics discussed in this resource should be observed in these Eucharistic liturgies.

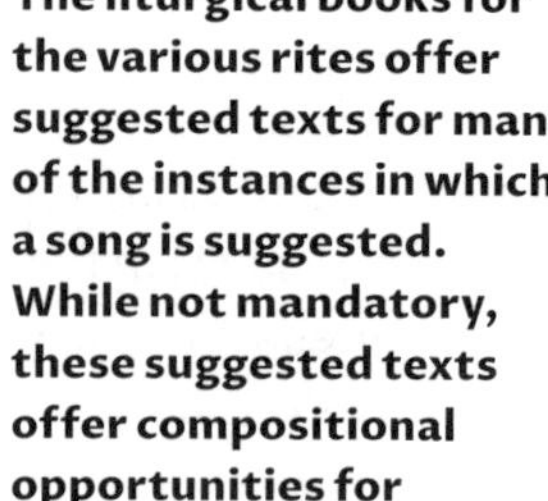

The liturgical books for the various rites offer suggested texts for many of the instances in which a song is suggested. While not mandatory, these suggested texts offer compositional opportunities for composers and, at the very least, indicate the nature of texts appropriate for specific moments in the rite.

—*Sing to the Lord: Music in Divine Worship*, 200

Christian Initiation of Adults

The Christian initiation process for adults includes a number of rituals customarily experienced within Sunday Mass with the gathered community. Many include the option for the assembly to join in singing psalms, acclamations, litanies, or other musical elements. Musical selections should be made in a way that enables and encourages the community's full participation in these rituals.[45]

Rite of Acceptance into the Order of Catechumens

This rite begins with the invitation for the assembly to join in: a song as the candidates, sponsors, and ministers gather outside the church; an acclamation as the candidates are marked with the sign of the cross; and a song or psalm during the entry to the church, before the Liturgy of the Word.

Rite of Sending for Election

The Rite of Election is normally celebrated on the First Sunday in Lent in the cathedral. Parishes may choose to formally send the catechumens forth from the community for their election. If the Book of the Elect is to be signed at the

45. Readers should note that at the time of this publication, a new translation of the *Rite of Christian Initiation of Adults* is pending approval from both the United States Conference of Catholic Bishops and the Vatican Congregation for Divine Worship. The title of this ritual will change to the *Order of Christian Initiation of Adults*. Please check on the status of this translation with your diocesan office of divine worship, your pastor, or director of liturgy.

parish and then later presented to the bishop, an acclamation may be sung at or after its signing by each catechumen.

The Three Scrutinies

The scrutinies are customarily celebrated on the Third, Fourth, and Fifth Sundays of Lent. The scrutinies themselves may be sung by the priest celebrant, and there is an option for a psalm or song at the end of the rite, following the exorcism.

Rites of Initiation (Easter Vigil)

Baptismal Liturgy: If your parish has elect who have been preparing for baptism, they are called forward and presented to the community following the homily. All will join in singing the Litany of Saints during the procession to the baptismal font. Additional saints' names may be added to the litany, such as name-saints for those to be baptized or the titular saint of the parish. Please note that some portions of the litany will be different if there are no baptisms to take place.

Following the prayer of blessing over the water, the cantor or choir may sing an acclamation of praise. It is especially helpful if this acclamation is musically connected (or identical) to the music you will use during the sprinkling rite or as a baptismal acclamation for each of the newly baptized. After the baptism(s), and the assembly's renewal of their baptismal promises, the entire assembly is sprinkled with holy water; the text is prescribed in the missal, although other "baptismally themed" options are acceptable.

Confirmation: If your parish is welcoming candidates into full communion with the Roman Catholic Church, confirmation takes place following the sprinkling rite. (If not, the elect would be anointed immediately following their baptism.) If you choose to have music during the laying on of hands and anointing with chrism, be careful that it does not obscure the ritual action or obliterate the words of the priest celebrant. A song may also be sung between the baptisms and confirmation.

After the rites of initiation are completed, the Mass continues with the Liturgy of the Eucharist.

Infant Baptism

Infant baptisms at Sunday Mass, although these may happen at other times of the year, are more frequent during Easter Time. When this happens, there are a few things of which the music minister should be aware:

The Gloria is sung when a baptism takes place during Mass. It is important that the music ministers be in good communication with the priest celebrant and the liturgy coordinators to clarify musical flow around the entrance song and Gloria.

The universal prayer may be chanted, and it concludes with the Litany of Saints (which replaces the usual concluding prayer).

Immediately following the baptism of the infant, the practice of the assembly singing a short acclamation together is encouraged.[46] Using the same acclamation for all parish baptisms (including the adult baptisms at the Easter Vigil) is helpful for linking these events in the minds of those gathered; the acclamation could be the refrain of the parish song at the sprinkling rite, or an acclamation expressly composed for this purpose, or even a simple alleluia refrain.

Matrimony

Celebrations of the marriage rite in parishes represent their own challenges within a parish setting. Since all couples will have varying levels of familiarity and comfort with the needs and flow of the liturgy, it is important that the parish and music ministers be able to assist and support couples in making their musical choices.

When the wedding is celebrated within Mass, all of the norms and characteristics discussed in this resource should be honored. This means that attention should be paid to the assembly's ability to participate in the prayers and songs, as well as to the couple's own personal musical preferences. A "soloist," if one is desired by the couple, should either be well versed and trained in the ministry of the cantor or a separate cantor and/or psalmist should be secured to meet the needs of the liturgy. Solo vocal moments should not replace or usurp musical moments or pieces where congregational singing is the norm. It goes without saying that secular music, whatever affection a particular song might hold for the couple, is not appropriate within the marriage liturgy (within Mass or during a Liturgy of the Word). Pastoral dialogue between the music minister(s), pastor, and bride and groom can be a wonderful opportunity for evangelization and catechesis regarding the distinct function and role played by music at each part of the celebration. The new translation of the *Order of Celebrating Matrimony* calls for a sung acclamation and congregational hymn during the marriage rite itself. Music ministers can help support and lead the assembly in this important participatory role.

Funerals

The funeral rite consists of three distinct parts, joined to one another by processions: the vigil for the deceased, the funeral liturgy, and the rite of committal. Music can and should play a significant role, especially in the first two of these parts, and may also be part of the rite of committal at the place of burial.

46. See OBC, 60.

Vigil for the Deceased

Music can play a pastoral and significant role in the vigil for the deceased. The presence of even one individual to serve in the ministry of cantor and lead the people in singing can be a wonderful part of this service. Within the structure of the vigil, there are several musical opportunities: The service has an opening song and a responsorial psalm, and it would also be appropriate to sing the prayers of intercession. None of the musical facets of the vigil need be complex or involved. Simple hymns accompanied or sung a cappella, Taizé-style ostinati, and chanted psalmody would work beautifully here.

The responsorial psalm specified in the *Order of Christian Funerals* is Psalm 27, although others may be used. Again, remember that it is not necessary to use a complicated setting of the psalm. Likewise, the intercessions can be chanted on a simple tone with a "Lord, have mercy" response in a melody familiar to the parish.

Remember to consider whether worship aids will be available to the gathered people. If even a simple aid is available under your parish reprint licenses, or a set of worship booklets can be purchased for this purpose, your choices are increased; if not, choose music your assembly can sing easily and without a worship aid.[47]

If there is access to a keyboard instrument (piano or organ), having someone to lead the singing can also be helpful. Take care, though, to ensure that there is sufficient musical leadership *in the midst* of the gathered people (some funeral homes have a single central organ in a small room, with piped sound into the various visitation rooms, a completely inadequate arrangement for leading assembly song) to facilitate the people's singing. Consider also the possibility of using a single woodwind or string instrument to lead the singing at a smaller service. You might think automatically that a keyboard or guitar is the only option for instrumental leadership, but a solo flute or cello, for example, can also give solid leadership—and is more portable.

The Funeral Liturgy

Of all parts of the funeral Mass (or even a funeral outside of Mass), it is often the music and the choice of songs that people remember for years. Many parishes are blessed with the ministry of a choir, made up frequently of retired parishioners and others with flexible schedules, whose members can be available with only a day or two's notice to provide musical leadership at funerals. Particularly for smaller gatherings, this presence is not only a gift of music but also a visible and aural demonstration of the support the people of a parish give to their beloved friends who have gone before them.

47. As a general rule for hospitality and evangelizing on the important role of liturgical participation, worship aids should be made available whenever there is assembly singing.

Sensitivity to the deep feelings being experienced by grieving family members and respect for the often overwhelming number of tasks they face calls for great flexibility. Remember that most of these families have probably never taken part in preparing a liturgy of any kind, let alone at such an emotional time. Producing written materials and repertoire list can be helpful in this process and can often be treated side by side with the preparation of the rest of the liturgy even by a nonmusician if the music minister cannot be part of the process. A basic repertoire familiar to the parish assemblies and music ministers, a simple outline of the different parts of the liturgy that call for music and the pastoral meaning behind each of those moments, and some suggestions for each part of the liturgy can make a family's job much easier. Some families may wish to select all of the music within the funeral Mass with great care; others may simply indicate a song or two that meant a great deal to the deceased. Some will have no musical preferences at all. Service music and psalmody should, to whatever extent possible, be drawn from the regular Sunday repertoire of the parish and be familiar and common to those gathered.

Preparing for Worship and Building Skills

The call to a new song can also be heard as a reminder to musicians to keep their art fresh. We all have a duty to become better at our musical skills.

The time you spend in practice is time you spend in private to prepare for public worship. It has the same value as daily prayers at home that anticipate Sunday prayer at church. Your practice time is sacred too. In it you come to know the music, yourself, God, and faith. In the quiet moments of practice you know how good the music can be. It warms your spirit.

When you come to Mass on Sunday to lead the music, you bring with you the experience of the practice room. You come with confidence. You come with a vision of what the music can be. You come with renewed faith, and you reveal it to the gathered assembly.

Good liturgical musicians will build their skills as well as their repertoire. You do not have to be a professional to lead the music at church. You have to be willing to share the gifts you have and willing to improve them as best you can. You come to church in the spirit of Peter and John, who came to the temple one day at the three o'clock hour and discovered a man crippled from birth asking them for alms. "Peter said, 'I have neither silver nor gold, but what I do have I give you: in the name of Jesus Christ the Nazorean, [rise and] walk.'"[48] If you wish to bring healing and life to those who gather at the church, you don't have to bring the silver and gold of professional musicianship. You bring what you have. With your gift those who languish will rise and walk.

48. Acts of the Apostles 3:6.

You will inspire people not just when you sing and play but also by your demeanor throughout the Mass. When you are attentive, they will be too. When you observe silence, so will they. If you are in view of others at Mass, it is important that you be a good model of worship from start to finish. Have the music handy so you do not create a distraction when you set it up. Do not change music during the readings or prayers. Be careful when you stand up from and sit down on the organ bench. Avoid giving directions to the choir during Mass if these can be given before. You are there not just as a musician but first as a member of the assembly. First, you worship with the community, and then within the community you exercise your role as a musician.

The ideal choir is one that is constantly attentive at prayer throughout the Mass, whether or not they may be seen by others. Choir members owe it to one another to create a spiritual space where all members can pray, listen, and make the responses during the Mass. You are all there to worship, not just to supply music at an occasional cue.

It is highly desirable that organists and other musicians should not only possess the skill to play properly the instrument entrusted to them: they should also enter into and be thoroughly aware of the spirit of the liturgy, so that even when playing ex tempore, they will enrich the sacred celebration according to the true nature of each of its parts, and encourage the participation of the faithful.

—*Musicam sacram*, 67

Warming Up

You owe it to your instrument (and yourself) to prepare your voice and body for the work it needs to do, if you are to do it well and without doing damage. Vocalists must awaken their vocal instruments, pianists and guitarists should take some time to get their fingers moving, and wind players should make sure they've blown enough warm air through their instrument for it to sound true and in tune. All musicians need to take time to work out the morning kinks in their primary instrument: the human body. No one should ever attempt any kind of physical exertion (the fine-motor exertion of playing an instrument is no exception—the current epidemic of carpal tunnel syndrome among computer users is a testament to this) without doing some form of basic stretching beforehand to awaken and limber the musculature.

Prepare

As part of your preparation, it is also important to consider the host of technical and organizational details involved in being ready for worship. If you don't want the old cliché "the Devil's in the details" to come true, then you need to be in the details first.

Choirs and Cantors

Before you begin any preliturgy rehearsal, before you even go to bed the night before, take the time to put your music in order. Cantors and psalmists should always have their music in a binder (no loose sheets of paper!). If you use hymnals, marker ribbons or small colored tabs can be used to mark each hymn or song to be sung that day (with the song title, number, and part of the liturgy when it will occur written on the visible part); this will save you from needing to flip wildly for the correct page. The small investment of time before the liturgy will reap great rewards both in your ability to make music and your freedom to truly pray and involve yourself in the liturgy without worrying about pages or music—you can simply be and do what you are there to do.

Instrumentalists

The same advice given for singers holds true for instruments as well, only even more so: have your music in order and clearly marked before you come to church the day of a liturgy. Be aware of potential page-turn problems and figure out solutions ahead of time. Tune your instrument (naturally this will not apply to pianos or organs, which are tuned seasonally) well before liturgy starts or, even better, tune it twice: once when you arrive and a second time about ten minutes before the liturgy begins after you are well warmed up. If the music you are using is confusing to follow (especially obbligato instrument parts), mark your music in pencil—clearly—so that you won't be confused when the actual moment arrives during the liturgy. If you are improvising a part, remember that even improvisation needs solid rehearsal. Know ahead of time where the improvisational passages will occur and have in your head at least some idea of what you plan to do.

Electronics

Added to the other details involved in preparing to serve as music ministers, the technological age now requires us to throw miles of microphone cords and power strips into the equation, to get tangled up in mixing boards, amplifiers, and microphone stands with oversized feet. A detailed discussion of optimal electronic amplification for music ministers is far beyond the scope of this book; still, some brief comments on commonsense ways to diminish potential problems might be helpful.

Some worship spaces, particularly those constructed before artificial amplification was available, were architecturally created to optimize projection of naturally produced sound. Choir lofts, while possessing significant pastoral disadvantages around the choir's ability to participate and feel like members of the assembly, often were designed so that the sound would move with ease, unamplified, down the nave of the church. If you minister in such a space and your musical ensembles tend to utilize music well-served by this gentle and natural acoustic, then you can very likely ignore this next section. Most of us, however, are faced with issues of amplification, and seldom do we consider just how much impact our use of technology has on our ministry's effectiveness.

Whatever microphone setup you use, prepare it well before the liturgy begins. Make sure there are several people who know how the system works, so that things can still be gotten together with minimal difficulty even on a Sunday when the primary "tech crew" person might be absent. Take the little extra time needed to keep extra loops of cord and power strips well out of the way and not underfoot; it looks much neater, and it decreases the likelihood of someone tripping. Make certain that everyone who handles the microphones, cords, and all other sound equipment knows how to take care of them gently and without abuse.

Rhythm instrument players who use their own amplifiers should likewise make sure that their equipment is set up well before the liturgy begins and that it does not conflict with any of the other parish sound equipment or present a tripping hazard.

Sometimes the setup is more complicated: Those who minister in situations with complex combinations of solo microphones, choir microphones, numerous amplified instruments, or a sound-mixing board should seek out an individual willing to take on the position of "sound engineer" as its own ministry. This person could have the responsibility of operating the mixing board for the music ministers throughout the liturgy, ready to adjust and monitor the sound at all times to make sure everything is being heard to its best advantage. On the other hand, most groups can get by with a simple setup, with all instruments' and singers' sound levels set prior to the liturgy. In this case, it is important for all the musicians (both vocal and instrumental) to know how to work with the microphones and adjust themselves to make the sound work best, rather than adjusting the microphones. As always, make certain all is in place well before the liturgy begins. Whenever your group is adjusting to a new or different sound situation, make certain you rehearse the sound equipment just as you would rehearse a new piece of music; give it the time it needs so that, in liturgy, it will serve the music rather than impede it. The best microphone setups will be the ones that permit music ministers to perform their ministry as though the microphones were not there at all; live music, after all, should look and sound like live music, not like a studio recording session. If the technology gets between the music ministry and the assembly in a way that separates or distances the two, something has gone wrong.

Rehearsal

Most music ministers, even having attended a full rehearsal earlier in the week, will take some time prior to the liturgy to warm up together and rehearse that day's music. Everything should not need to be practiced. A touch-up on anything that felt difficult at the end of the week's rehearsal, a solid run-through of any choir-only music, and a talk-through of any potentially confusing parts of the liturgy should be sufficient. This rehearsal should always end with plenty of time (ten to fifteen minutes at least) to enable ministers to quiet themselves and prepare inwardly for the liturgy. This space of time, as we have mentioned before, should not be spent practicing, setting up microphones, doing sound checks, or any other such activities (with the exception of one final tuning for instrumentalists). Musical and technical preparation should already be done; now it is time for personal and spiritual preparation. Furthermore, during their time of preparation for worship, the members of the assembly should not hear the music of the day being rehearsed before its use in the liturgy.

Some musical groups, especially those in parishes that are widely spread out geographically or that involve many extremely busy high school or young-adult-aged music ministers, find it easier to hold the weekly rehearsal on Sunday immediately before the liturgy, rather than scheduling practice on a separate day. This can work very well; however, in a situation like this there needs to be all the more diligence regarding before-liturgy preparation. It is too tempting to take that extra five minutes to sharpen something musically (or cover something that didn't get covered earlier in the practice) and wind up rehearsing until four minutes before the liturgy begins. This is fair neither to the music ministers nor to the gathered assembly. Make certain that some transition time is built into your schedule, so that everyone can be fully ready—mentally, physically, and spiritually—to minister to the best of his or her ability and gifts. It will work best, if possible, if rehearsals before the liturgy do not take place in the worship space.

Care of the Human Instrument (for Singers)

Any instrument needs good care and regular preventive maintenance; the vocal instrument is no exception. Complicating this issue is the reality that you cannot easily examine your instrument for stress or damage except based on how you feel at any given moment. Medications that correct one set of symptoms can have a negative effect on the voice itself. Therefore preventive maintenance is by far the best route to pursue—take care of your body, head to toe, and your vocal instrument will in most cases take care of itself. You have heard it all before, many times: eat a sensible and balanced diet; avoid excessive caffeine, refined sugars and starches, and alcohol. Exercise regularly. Get plenty of rest. Avoid stress; mental and emotional anxiety have profound and immediate effects on the body in general and tend to manifest very quickly in the voice and throat area. Be aware of how you use your voice in non-singing situations; the best vocal singing technique can be completely undone by abuse of the vocal cords and poor vocal speaking technique. Above all, stay well hydrated, all the time, not just when you are singing. It cannot be stressed too much: we cannot care for our voices without caring for our whole selves.

Continuing to Learn

Whether you are new to the music ministry or have been involved in this kind of music making for decades, it is important that you continue to grow and learn. If you have never taken private lessons, consider trying it for a while, or try taking some continuing education classes in music at a local college. If you have any interest in other genres of music than what you play or sing in church, explore them. Challenge yourself to always improve your skills.

Instrumentalists who can sight-read anything put before them might consider specifically working to develop improvisational skills. Singers and instrumentalists who have always learned by ear would highly benefit by entering the process of learning to read music. The ability to work out how one's piece of music should sound fosters independence and confidence and saves a tremendous amount of time and work when learning a piece of music.

Spiritual Growth

The above addresses musical growth and learning; but that's only the tip of the iceberg. Your spirit needs tending as well. Go on retreat whenever you can, even if it's only a few hours once every few months. Participate in faith-sharing groups if you are able. Learn all you can about the way liturgy works and how our worship came to develop over time into the shape it now holds. Read the Church's documents on liturgy and music so that you'll better understand why we do the things we do. Spend some time with each Sunday's readings and reflect on them before you prepare your music for that week. Look at the symbols in your worship space; listen to the ancient texts. Tune yourself to the underlying rhythms and flow of the liturgy itself. It has its own song, as beautiful as any symphony ever written. When you enter into it, you begin to perceive your own musical moments as small but crucial phrases in a music that began two thousand years ago and shows no end in sight. What a joy and privilege it is to carry forward this beautiful song and to teach and empower our brothers and sisters to do the same!

When we gather for worship, we gather to proclaim Christ who was born among us, died for love of us, and rose from the dead—Christ who sent the Holy Spirit to us that we might truly be his Body in the world. Just as we tend to our art and our skills, we tend to our faith, that our loving God—Father, Son, and Holy Spirit—might be known and celebrated in gratitude and generosity and hope. We pray, and we work, and we struggle, and we grow . . . and we sing.

Questions for Discussion and Reflection

1. What does your musical life outside the liturgy look like? Do you have the opportunity to sing and make music in family and social settings as well as in church? What are those opportunities like?

2. Who are some of your favorite composers, songwriters, and singers (liturgical or otherwise)? What about their music inspires you?

3. When you are at liturgy but not serving as a music minister, what happens for you? What is the experience like? How does being a "person in the pew" as opposed to a music minister affect your experience of the liturgy?

4. What feelings or emotions do the words *performer* and *prayer* bring out in you?

5. What is your favorite piece of liturgical music? What about that particular piece do you love so much? Is it the text, the melody, the feelings you have when singing it, a memory associated with it, or some other factor or factors that draw you to it?

Chapter Four

Spirituality and Discipleship

O Trinity, you are music, you are life.

—St. Hildegard of Bingen

"Like other baptized members of the assembly, pastoral musicians need to hear the Gospel, experience conversion, profess faith in Christ, and so proclaim the praise of God."[1] With this statement, *Sing to the Lord* rightfully acknowledges that faith, not talent, is the starting point of ministry. Without this acknowledgment, music ministers risk becoming merely performers. A musician could possess all the talent in the world and have degrees from the finest musical conservatories, however, if their faith is lacking or not present in their life, it would be difficult to qualify that person as a music minister. The faith is passed on to us when we are baptized. Baptism commits us to a life of service in the Lord by using the gifts God gave us.

St. Paul reminds us that each of us has different gifts from God.[2] Jesus also reminds us that we are the light of the world and that we should let our lights shine before others.[3] Being part of a parish music ministry is not just a volunteer opportunity to use our talents. It is a true vocation, a calling from God to build up the Church and, as the Gospel according to Matthew reminds us, to "glorify your heavenly Father."[4] Pope St. John Paul II encourages us not to waste our God-given talents but to develop them for the good of society.[5] The Jesuit spiritual writer Pedro Arrupe, SJ, develops this idea of the artistic vocation of music ministers:

> More than the preacher's word, it is the musician's touch that is bringing the young to God again. More than the politician, it is the folk singer who draws the races hand in hand. Heart speaks to heart in mysterious ways, and it is the artist that holds the key to the mystery.[6]

It is often said that people don't usually leave Mass humming the homily, but how often do people leave humming the favorite hymn they just sang? Music ministry is an opportunity for evangelization, and the music of the liturgy reaches deep into the human soul to places where words alone cannot reach.

The *General Instruction of the Roman Missal*, the document that sets forth the guidelines for the celebration of Mass, reminds us that in baptism we

---

1. STL, 49.
2. See 1 Corinthians 7:7.
3. See Matthew 5:14–16.
4. Matthew 5:15.
5. See *Letter to Artists*, 3.
6. *Studies in the Spirituality of Jesuits* 5, no. 3 (1973): 91.

are called to participate in offering the Mass, alongside and with the priest. At Mass, we form a "holy people" so that we "may give thanks to God and offer the unblemished sacrificial Victim . . . together with him."[7] The *General Instruction* goes on to remind us that we participate in the offering by showing charity to those who are at Mass with us.[8] We show charity when we offer our seat to a stranger or give a smile to the person sitting next to us that we've never seen at Mass before.

The idea that that we participate in the offering of the Mass is often overlooked. Yet every time we gather for Mass, we sing one of three acclamations following the institution narrative. These acclamations remind us that we participate in the offering. Directed to Christ himself, these acclamations give us a powerful voice at the heart of the Mass, the Eucharistic Prayer, and remind us that we participate in the offering. In addition, during the Eucharistic Prayer, the priest often uses the plural word *we* when referring to who is offering the prayer.

When a new music minister is introduced to the community, it is appropriate to use the *Order of Blessing Servers, Sacristans, Musicians and Ushers* from the *Book of Blessings*. One of the intercessions in the ritual reminds us that all the baptized participate in the offering: "For the Church of Christ and for this parish of N., that all Christians may offer themselves as living sacrifices, we pray to the Lord."[9]

When we eat this Bread and drink this Cup, we proclaim your Death, O Lord, until you come again.

—Memorial Acclamation

So, what does all this mean for music ministers and what difference does it make in how we sing and make music at Mass? Primarily, it reminds us of the importance of our actions and our attentiveness to the celebration of Mass. It also means remaining attentive to the Scripture readings, prayers, and homily and actively making the responses to the different dialogues of the Mass. It is very easy to tune out during the readings or be tempted to check our phones during the homily. This can be particularly challenging for music ministers who are often at multiple Masses on a given weekend. Understanding that all the baptized participate in the offering of Mass leads us to a whole new mind-set and shifts our frame of reference.

One of the benefits of being part of the music ministry is the opportunity to interact with other parishioners. This is a reminder that in baptism, we are welcomed into the Catholic Christian community and are part of something much larger than ourselves. St. Paul often refers to the Church as the Body of Christ.[10] As a member of the Body of Christ, this means that the work of a

7. GIRM, 95.
8. See GIRM, 95.
9. *Book of Blessings*, 1853.
10. See Philippians 2:1–5.

minister is never done in isolation but rather with and among other people. They also remind us that ministry is not about us but about serving others.

As with any form of human interaction, serving in music ministry can be both a blessing and a burden. It can be a blessing when there are healthy group dynamics present, when boundaries are established and respected, and when communication is good. It can be a burden when the group dynamics are unhealthy, when boundaries are unknown or crossed, or when communication is lacking. Church ministries often attract people who have great needs, either physical, spiritual, or emotional. Sometimes conflicts arise in choirs because of human nature or tension between people. This can be amplified in choirs or ensembles where the same group of people usually gathers or interacts on a frequent basis. A good music director or leader is often able to diffuse tension and maintain peace and order in the group. Sometimes, conflict is heightened because of the busyness of the liturgical season or the demands of the calendar. At other times it can be heightened by personal egos or by poor or ineffective leadership of the music ministry. Perhaps that is why St. Paul admonishes us:

Let us sing a new song not with our lips but with our lives.

—St. Augustine

> Put on then, as God's chosen ones, holy and beloved, heartfelt compassion, kindness, humility, gentleness, and patience, bearing with one another and forgiving one another, if one has a grievance against another; as the Lord has forgiven you, so must you also do. And over all these put on love, that is, the bond of perfection. And let the peace of Christ control your hearts, the peace into which you were also called in one body. And be thankful.[11]

Questions for Discussion and Reflection

1. How often do you reflect on your baptismal call?
2. How do you envision your role within the Christian assembly?
3. Are you using the gifts and charisms given to you at baptism for the service of the Church and world?
4. How does the music you sing or play challenge people to think about how they participate in the offering of the Mass?

Ministry Rooted in the Word of God

At every liturgical celebration—whether it is Mass, the Liturgy of the Hours, or the celebration of one of the sacraments or rituals—the Church proclaims

11. Colossians 3:12–15.

the Scriptures, and the voice of God is heard. Because a good deal of Catholic liturgy is scripturally based, music ministers are immersed in the Word of God. Beyond the four Scripture passages that are typically proclaimed at Sunday Mass, Scripture texts are used throughout the Order of Mass: in the entrance and Communion antiphons; in the verse before the Gospel; in the ritual music like the Gloria, the Holy, Holy, Holy, and the Lamb of God; as well as in our treasury of hymns, both ancient and modern. Two examples include "This Is the Feast of Victory" by Richard Hillert, which is paraphrased from the Book of Revelation, and "Unless a Grain of Wheat" by Bernadette Farrell, which is based on John 12:24. Even many choral anthems and major choral works are based on the texts of the Scriptures. Handel's choral masterpiece *Messiah* is a commentary on Christ's nativity, passion, resurrection, and ascension, beginning with God's promises as spoken by the prophets and ending with Christ's glorification in heaven.

The *General Instruction* states: "When the Sacred Scriptures are read in the Church, God himself speaks to his people, and Christ, present in his word, proclaims the Gospel."[12] The fourth option of the dismissal of Mass even challenges to "go and announce the Gospel of the Lord." The People of God are nourished at two tables at Mass: "at the table of the Lord's body"[13] *and* at "the table of God's word."[14] The ambo where the Scriptures are proclaimed is also a table where we feast, and what we receive there is Christ himself, since "he is present in his word, since it is he himself who speaks when the holy Scriptures are read in the Church."[15]

The Word that we encounter at liturgy is not just a historical record of the Church, the life of Christ, or the account of ancient Israel. While the Scriptures were written at a particular moment in history within a particular cultural context, they are the living Word of God and speak to us here and now. Thus, they are both universal and timeless. The Word of God is not just the domain of the clergy or the readers who proclaim the readings—it is for all the baptized. St. Jerome, one of the earliest translators of the Bible, once famously said, "Ignorance of Scriptures is ignorance of Christ."[16]

Find new ways to spread the word of God to every corner of the world.

—Pope Francis

The traditional monastic spiritual exercise called *lectio divina* involves the slow and deliberate reading of Scriptures, followed by meditation and prayer to promote communion with God and to increase the knowledge

12. GIRM, 29.
13. SC, 48.
14. GIRM, 57.
15. SC, 7.
16. From the prologue of the commentary on Isaiah by St. Jerome as included in the Office of Readings for the Memorial of St. Jerome.

Music ministers should make an effort to read and reflect on the Scripture readings for the upcoming Sunday, particularly the responsorial psalm and Gospel.

and understanding of God's Word. This practice could effectively be taught to music ministers to help them appreciate the richness of the Scriptures.

Music ministers should make an effort to read and reflect on the Scripture readings for the upcoming Sunday, particularly the responsorial psalm and Gospel. When you come to Mass familiar with the readings, you can be more open to hearing connections or nuances that you might not notice if you hear the Scriptures for the first time at Mass. When you are prepared to listen, different passages may strike you and you might notice connections that you may not have been aware of before.

Having a Catholic Bible in the home is a good practice. A larger and more beautifully designed family Bible could even be out in a common area and used for more formal prayer settings while a smaller study Bible could be kept at the bedside or on a nightstand for quicker reference. If it helps to write notes in the Bible itself or in a journal, that should be considered. Take time to get to know the Bible and to learn about the various characters God called and used in his plan of salvation. Some of those characters were ordinary people like you and me. Remember, God doesn't always call the equipped, but he equips those whom he calls.[17]

The preparatory document for the 2008 Synod of Bishops on "The Word of God in the Life and Mission of the Church" urges us to use every means at our disposal to proclaim the Gospel, including "radio, TV, theatre, cinema, music and songs, including the more recent media, such as CDs, DVDs,

17. A Catholic Bible has to have what is known as a *nihil obstat*, a declaration from the bishop's office of the diocese where it is published that confirms that the Bible does not contain anything morally or doctrinally objectionable. It also must contain an *imprimatur* or official approval by the bishop's office. A Catholic Bible also must include the entire Biblical canon, the body of books approved by the Church. There are certain books that are part of the Catholic canon that are not included in the Bibles of some other Christian denominations such as Tobit, Judith, Baruch, Sirach, 1 Maccabees, 2 Maccabees, Wisdom, and parts of the Books of Esther, Baruch, and Daniel.

Internet, etc."[18] There are a number of apps for smartphones and tablets that give us immediate access to the Bible. The website of the United States Conference of Catholic Bishops has an entire section devoted to the Bible and offers an opportunity to subscribe to see the readings of the day, to listen to them in a podcast or video, or even to have them emailed to you.[19]

In 2019, Pope Francis invited the Church to set aside the Second Sunday in Ordinary Time to reflect specifically on the Word of God:

> Devoting a specific Sunday of the liturgical year to the word of God can enable the Church to experience anew how the risen Lord opens up for us the treasury of his word and enables us to proclaim its unfathomable riches before the world.[20]

Music ministers ought to take advantage of this annual opportunity to reflect on the centrality of the Scriptures, not only in the Church's communal worship, but also in the hearts of all believers.

Questions for Discussion and Reflection

1. How aware are you of the importance of the Scriptures in the liturgy?
2. Do you spend time with the Scriptures and ultimately spend time with Christ?
3. As a member of the music ministry, do you consider yourself a proclaimer of the Word of God?
4. When was the last time you opened your Bible?

Prayer

Pope St. John Paul II once wrote about the importance of forming parishioners in prayer, a formation that he noted is central to parish life:

> Our Christian communities must become *genuine "schools" of prayer*, where the meeting with Christ is expressed not just in imploring help but also in thanksgiving, praise, adoration, contemplation, listening and ardent devotion, until the heart truly "falls in love."[21]

Music ministers, as parish liturgical ministers and public witnesses, are important "students" in this school of prayer and must believe, profess, and live the words that are sung in the liturgy, otherwise their ministry risks becoming an empty show.

18. *Lineamenta* for the Synod on the Word of God in the Life and Mission of the Church, 26.
19. Refer to www.usccb.org.
20. *Aperuit illis*, 2.
21. *Novo millennio inuente*, 33.

A parish's music ministry should have ample time for communal prayer, either at the beginning or the end of the regular rehearsal times. This can be led by the director or a rotation of other music ministers. Allowing time for people to share their prayer intentions is always a good segue into the prayer itself. Some find that a prayer focused on the Gospel for the upcoming Sunday works well for them. Others adapt Evening Prayer or Night Prayer from the Liturgy of the Hours, the Church's official daily prayer.

Attention to individual prayer is an important consideration as well. Think about attending daily Mass, especially as a participant in the assembly without any assigned musical role or praying the Liturgy of the Hours, the Rosary, or the Stations of the Cross. Consider participating in an annual retreat or days of reflection at your parish or a local retreat center. You can also benefit by seeking out spiritual direction from a parish leader trained in that practice to help guide your prayer life. Consider spending time in the presence of the Blessed Sacrament outside of Mass. Stop and pray before the tabernacle before or after Mass or both. Try to take advantage of times for Eucharistic adoration, either in the tabernacle or exposed in a monstrance. This is a way for us to contemplate the Eucharistic mystery that calls the many into one and incorporates us into Christ's Body, the Church.

Ultimately, prayer must lead us to a deeper relationship with Christ so that we can serve his Body, the Church, more effectively. Before an airplane departs from the gate at the airport, the flight attendant reminds those flying that if the oxygen masks are deployed, one should fit the mask on one's own face before helping a child, or anyone else, with their mask. Similarly, those leading prayer must first be people who are immersed in prayer. Our prayer may not always be perfect, as the distractions and conditions of human living often get in the way. But our prayer must always be sincere, genuine, and rooted in a desire to draw deeper to Christ.

Among our tasks as witnesses to the love of Christ is that of giving voice to the cry of the poor.

—Pope Francis

Attention to silence is an important part of developing a healthy prayer life even though our society seems to be uncomfortable with it. Our society tends to have a yearning to fill every second of the day with some kind of noise or activity. The screen-time reminder on our smartphones can be a chilling reminder of our aversion to silence. Yet if we don't empty ourselves so that we can truly listen to the Lord speaking to us, we might miss a golden opportunity. It is no mere coincidence that the words LISTEN and SILENT contain the same letters, albeit in a different arrangement. We can't truly listen unless we are silent, and we can't truly be silent unless we listen. This reminds us that prayer is a two-way street that involves communication between God and us. How often do we limit our definition of prayer to us talking to God or asking God to heal someone or give us wisdom to do the right thing or to make the right decision? Authentic prayer demands that we surrender ourselves over to the will of God. To do that, we first have to empty our minds and be silent so that God can speak to us.

Pope Emeritus Benedict XVI reminds:

> Silent contemplation immerses us in the source of that Love who directs us towards our neighbors so that we may feel their suffering and offer them the light of Christ, his message of life and his saving gift of the fullness of love. In silent contemplation, then, the eternal Word, through whom the world was created, becomes ever more powerfully present and we become aware of the plan of salvation that God is accomplishing throughout our history by word and deed.[22]

In the sacred silence of the first Holy Saturday, Jesus lay in the tomb, awaiting what was to be the penultimate moment of his ministry, his resurrection from the dead.[23] Imagine what can happen to us if we truly surrender ourselves over to him in complete and utter silence?

Questions for Discussion and Reflection

1. How does your prayer help you focus to be a better music minister?
2. What forms of individual prayer are more meaningful to you than others?
3. Is your prayer life regular and intentional?
4. Are you able to encounter God in silence?

Daily Christian Living

Music ministers are called to go out into the world living what they just sang about. Witnessing to the dying and rising of Christ Jesus is the business of all Christian disciples in the world, in homes and workplaces and among friends, coworkers, and everyone we encounter and interact with. One of the greatest challenges of living the Christian life is moving beyond seeing the Mass as our only encounter with holiness. If our experience of Sunday worship is truly authentic, we should be able to see our lives as a continuation and extension of what we experience at the celebration of the Eucharist. Ultimately, you are not just playing the role of music minister; you are also living the role as a missionary disciple. If you nourish yourself with sincere prayer, engage in the liturgical act and live an authentic Christian life, you are giving yourself the nourishment you need to live the role.

---

22. Message for the Forty-Sixth World Communications Day: Silence and Word; Path of Evangelization. Sunday, May 20, 2012.

23. The last moment being his ascension to the right hand of God, forty days after his resurrection.

Pope Francis reminds us of our duty to put on Christ as missionary disciples in the new evangelization:

> In virtue of their baptism, all the members of the People of God have become missionary disciples (see Matthew 28:19). All the baptized, whatever their position in the Church or their level of instruction in the faith, are agents of evangelization, and it would be insufficient to envisage a plan of evangelization to be carried out by professionals while the rest of the faithful would simply be passive recipients. The new evangelization calls for personal involvement on the part of each of the baptized. Every Christian is challenged, here and now, to be actively engaged in evangelization.[24]

This is a clarion call for those who sing the Word of God to live the Word of God.

Music ministers might participate in group service projects to reinforce the missionary aspect of their ministry. Perhaps the music ministry might "adopt a family" at Thanksgiving and Christmas, have a food drive for the parish food pantry, or go to a local nursing home to sing for the residents. Maybe the proceeds from a concert might go to Catholic Charities, a local home for single mothers, or a halfway house for those preparing to reenter society after a time of incarceration. Even the way we care for fellow music ministers in need reflects our missionary zeal.

Christ has no body now but yours.
No hands, no feet on earth but yours.
Yours are the eyes through which he ooks compassion on this world.
Yours are the feet with which he walks to do good.
Yours are the hands through which he blesses all the world.
Yours are the hands, yours are the feet, yours are the eyes, you are his body.
Christ has no body now on earth but yours.

—St. Teresa of Avila

We come to the celebration of the Eucharist not only to fulfill an obligation but, more importantly, to be transformed, to become more like Christ. That is our call as music ministers, as disciples of Christ, and as stewards of the gifts God gave us when we were baptized. Just as the bread and wine presented at Mass are transformed into Christ's own Body and Blood, so too are we transformed to become more like Christ. Reflecting on that call to transformation is a challenge for us when we live in a society that seems to encourage us to take care of ourselves first.

The English word *Mass* actually comes from the final words of the Mass in Latin, "*Ite missa est*," which is literally translated as, "Go, you are sent." This reminds us that the Mass is an action, a verb, a command. When we are dismissed from Mass, we are sent to go forth to "become what we receive," as St. Augustine reminds us, to become the Body of Christ. We are called to

24. *Evangelii gaudium*, 120.

live a life congruent with what we just celebrated. So, it is not only the reception of the Eucharist but also the living out of the Eucharistic life that makes us holy.

The words of one of the prefaces of the Eucharistic Prayer remind us that "we approach the table of this wondrous Sacrament, / so that, bathed in the sweetness of your grace, / we may pass over to the heavenly realities here foreshadowed."[25] This is participation in what is called the paschal mystery—the dying and rising of Christ. We grow into the likeness of the risen Christ when we become Christ to other people. When we stay up at night with one of our sick children, or when we assist our neighbor suffering with an addiction, or when we share our hearts with a family mourning the loss of a loved one, we participate in Christ's paschal mystery. In music ministry, you participate in the paschal mystery when you commit yourself to weekly rehearsals and liturgies on Sundays and holidays when you are called away from your families and loved ones, especially in the busy times like Christmas and Easter. You die and rise in Christ when you work for many weeks on that difficult choral piece or help your fellow singer who is struggling with the notes or can't find the right page. When age, health conditions, or pandemics restrict or even silence your voices, you unite yourself with Christ's suffering and death. Participation in Christ's paschal mystery is not simply an event of the past as it happens every day of our lives. When we help people connect to Christ's dying and rising by reflecting on their own dying and rising, then we are living out the Eucharistic life and we are, God willing, on the path to holiness.

True holiness means more than just reciting prayers, as authentic prayer should ultimately lead us to action. The great spiritual writer Thomas Merton tells us that "prayer is not only the lifting up of the mind and heart to God, but it is also the response to God within us, the discovery of God within us."[26] We respond to God's invitation by reaching out to others, especially those in need. What makes us truly holy is living out that prayer by the example and witness of our lives.

Questions for Discussion and Reflection

1. How is your life consistent with the words you sing as a member of the music ministry?
2. How does participating in the music ministry connect you to the wider Church?
3. What are some of the ways that you participate in and experience Christ's paschal mystery?

25. Preface II of the Most Holy Eucharist.

26. Quoted in William H. Shannon, *Thomas Merton's Paradise Journey: Writings on Contemplation* (Cincinnati: St. Anthony Messenger Press, 2000), 148.

Chapter Five

Frequently Asked Questions

1. Our church has a choir loft—why don't we use it anymore?

Like much of the music composed prior to the Second Vatican Council, many of the most beautiful and artfully constructed churches were designed not only for the preconciliar rites but also for a time when amplification technology was not available.

This is not necessarily a bad thing. Musicians at many preconciliar churches with choir lofts find that they are excellent vehicles for sending vibrant live sound down the nave and among the gathered faithful, giving the people in the pews a sense of real support—quite literally at their backs. There is no substitute for the warmth of live voices to help support and encourage other live voices. Good pastoral use of a choir loft, however, often presents other challenges.

Successful ministry from a choir loft requires good numbers of vocalists with strong projection, or no acoustics in the world will be able to give the sound enough body to do its job. Once electronic amplification is needed, the loft becomes a hindrance to good music ministry rather than a help. The warmth of living supportive sound is replaced by disembodied voices coming from a speaker. This disembodiment creates a distance and separation from the assembly far greater than simple geography: a music ministry heard and not seen or even kinesthetically "felt" within the room cannot truly be part of the assembly. For all the people in the pews know, the choir could be in another building.

Thus, almost all small ensembles or choirs, or those using almost any instrument other than the organ (in a best-case scenario, a pipe organ specifically designed, like the loft itself, to send warm and living sound down the nave of the church), will not be able to lead as successfully from a loft as they could from a placement in front or to the side of the assembly. Music ministers should ideally be in a place where their unamplified sound can permeate the room and where there can be some clear ear/eye connection between those making the sound and those who hear it.

Another challenge presented by use of most choir lofts, even in churches that are not large, is what to do with the cantor when the instrumental and choral music is coming from the back of the church. If the cantor performs his or her ministry from behind the people, the responsorial psalm is not properly proclaimed from the ambo, and gestures of leadership and support are useless because they are not seen. Thus the cantor normally sings in front of the worship space. However, it takes time for the sound of the organ to travel to the cantor and for the cantor's sound to travel back to the organist. This can produce frustration and lack of ensemble. Cantors who minister at a distance from the leading instrument have a far more difficult task—although not necessarily an insurmountable one—and need good solidity and practice.

There can be many reasons why a particular choir loft no longer contributes to a successful music ministry, or is less conducive than another placement. For example, the church may be too large or the assembly not large enough to achieve a sense of aural connection and support between choir and assembly. Consider also that renovations to the church may have resulted in carpeting or pew padding that further muffle the sound. In addition, the delay in sound being carried may be too great even for the most experienced cantors. Ultimately, this question, like so many others, goes back to the fundamental role of the music ministry: before all else you are to support and facilitate the assembly's song, wherever and however your particular circumstances best allow you to do that.

2. We're doing everything we should be doing—but sometimes (or all the time) the people just don't seem to be participating. What are we doing wrong?

We must never cease examining ourselves or assume that there's nothing we can do to make our ministry more effective. Of course, there are *many* factors involved in whether an assembly joins fully in the singing at liturgy on a particular day. A parish where singing is lackadaisical and unenthusiastic may take years of consistent and unflagging encouragement at *all* liturgies before it becomes a strong and singing parish. It is almost inevitable that, even with strong leadership, there will be ebb and flow. Even in parishes that already sing with strength, some days it just does not happen as we would like: the weather is bad, the parish school and religious education programs have a three-day weekend, the pastor has a cold—many things can have a negative effect on the singing on a particular day.

3. We know the four-part harmony of a lovely new entrance song, but our music director is telling us to sing it in unison. What's wrong? Does he or she think we can't handle it?

Very likely quite the contrary. Remember that your primary purpose, especially with a newer piece of music, is to enable and empower the *assembly* to sing well. In our current cultural climate, in which music is almost universally perceived as something to be created by the experts and listened to by everyone else, it is especially important that we avoid giving our assemblies any reason to think they should *stop* singing to listen to us. Unfortunately, that beautiful four-part hymn setting you know so well might tend to lull people into listening to you, rather than adding their voices to the song. No doubt, once the assembly is singing this hymn solidly and with strength, your music director will have you sing the harmony parts. There are, of course, moments when it is appropriate to listen in a prayerful manner to the choir's song. But the song that opens the liturgy should definitely defer to the assembly.

4. There are so many wonderful Masses by Mozart, Palestrina, and so many more composers. Why don't we ever sing them at liturgy?

The documents from the Second Vatican Council presented the norms for the reform and promotion of the liturgy. Subsequent legislation also has shaped the way that we celebrate communal worship. During these postconciliar decades, we, as a Church, have embraced the great value of full, active, and conscious participation by our gathered assemblies, especially during the parts of the liturgy that remain constant week after week. Of the preconciliar "ordinary" parts of the Mass (the Kyrie, Gloria, Credo, Sanctus, and Agnus Dei), the *General Instruction on the Roman Missal* provides for solo choir performance of only the Gloria.[1] Sadly, these marvelous Masses referred to above from our Church's heritage often are not suitable for assembly singing. Many music directors, however, are finding creative ways to use these gems from our heritage at other liturgical moments, without detracting from the participation of the people.

5. If the assembly kneels during the Eucharistic Prayer, should we also kneel? Or stand throughout the prayer?

This is a question for your music director to address with the pastor and members of the pastoral staff—the decision is then communicated to other liturgical ministers. The guiding principle should be: What posture distracts the assembly the least?

For the choir or vocal ensemble, it is normally easiest to simply stand, sit, and kneel along with the assembly; the acclamations sung during the Eucharistic Prayer should truly belong to the assembly and usually do not need much assistance. Vocal issues with harmonies or high-register descants, when applicable, can usually be negotiated with good posture, even in a kneeling position. If an instrumentalist is to play for the acclamations, he or she needs to be in a position where this is possible. The thing to consider here is what will best serve the assembly and keep the focus where it ought to be, on the presiding celebrant and the altar. If an organist or other instrumentalist cannot subtly move to and from the instrument to a kneeling position without

1. See GIRM, 53; even the Gloria would normally be sung by the priest, cantor, choir, and all the people together.

drawing attention to the movement, it is better to simply stay put at the instrument and thereby avoid distracting the assembly from the liturgical action.

6. I sing in the choir at the 9:30 AM Sunday Mass. I also play guitar for the youth ensemble during the 5:00 PM Sunday Mass. May I receive holy Communion at both Masses?

You may receive holy Communion at both Masses, provided that you participate fully during each liturgy. You may not receive a third time the same day.

7. When should I receive holy Communion?

The *General Instruction of the Roman Missal* specifies that the Communion song should begin *while* the priest celebrant receives the Sacrament, and the song should continue "for as long as the Sacrament is being administered to the faithful."[2] The same article also cautions, "Care should be taken that singers, too, can receive Communion with ease."[3] This can create a logistical conundrum for music ministers: when and how to receive holy Communion while also serving the assembly through the entire Communion Rite.

When the music ministry during the liturgy consists solely of a cantor and organist/pianist, options are limited. If the organist and cantor were to receive at the *beginning* of the Communion procession, the music would be delayed while the priest and extraordinary ministers receive holy Communion. This distorts the clear intention that the music for the Communion Rite starts at the beginning of holy Communion. It also could give the impression that the reception of holy Communion by the priest and ministers is a separate part of the rite, rather than a seamless piece of the whole. An added benefit of starting the song at the beginning of the rite, as the *General Instruction* specifies, is that a verse or two of the Communion song may begin while most of the people are still in their places. With the song or refrain already upon their lips, they are more likely to sing in the procession and after returning to their places.

The only logical time for the cantor's and organist's reception of holy Communion, then, is at the end of the procession. Coordination is important, so that the necessary extraordinary ministers of holy Communion know to wait for the musicians to finish the Communion song. The cantor and organist can receive immediately following the song and at the beginning of the time of silent private prayer after all have received.[4]

For liturgies where a choir is present in addition to the organist/pianist and cantor, there are more options, although any of these options takes coordination and preparation. As in any other liturgy, the song should begin while the priest receives the Sacrament. The cantor could start the song *with* the

2. GIRM, 86.
3. GIRM, 86.
4. See GIRM, 88.

choir, and the choir go to receive holy Communion by sections or all together, while the cantor maintains vocal leadership. Once all choristers have returned to their places and taken up the song, the cantor receives holy Communion. In parishes with vibrant assembly singing, this can be done when there is no choir; the cantor brings in the people on the final refrain and *leaves* the cantor stand as the assembly continues singing. This can convey a powerful message and affirmation of the importance of the assembly's voice and the *true* role of the cantor in empowering the song of the people.

If your ensemble has instruments in addition to the keyboard, especially guitars, the instrumentalists can take turns supporting the singing while the others receive holy Communion; the guitarist and bassist can receive while the piano supports the sound. Once they return and take up playing, the pianist can receive. Alternatively, a musically beautiful and effective technique, particularly with a full four-part choir, is to invite all to sing the final refrain a cappella, thus enabling instrumentalists to receive holy Communion *and* allowing the assembly to hear its harmonically embellished voice unsupported by instruments.

Appendix

Care of the Human Voice

Care of the Human Voice

Suggestions for Healthy Singing

- **Eat a balanced diet.**
- **Avoid caffeine, refined sugar and starches, dairy, and alcohol.**
- **Keep physically fit.**
- **Avoid stress.**
- **Drink lots of water.**
- **Warm up.**

Of all musicians, singers are the ones whose instrument is a part of the body and not an external contraption of metal or wood. Any instrument needs good care and regular preventative maintenance; the vocal instrument is no exception. Complicating this issue is the reality that we cannot easily examine the inner workings of the instrument for stress or damage; all we can do is evaluate based on how we feel at any given moment. Medications to treat illnesses, effective as they may be for their intended purpose, sometimes have a negative effect on the voice itself. Therefore, preventative maintenance is by far the best route to take—take care of your body, head to toe, and your vocal instrument will in most cases take care of itself. You have doubtless heard it before, many times: Eat a sensible and balanced diet, and avoid excessive caffeine, refined sugars and starches, and alcohol. Exercise regularly. Get plenty of rest. Avoid stress. Mental and emotional anxieties have profound and immediate effects on the body in general and tend to manifest very quickly in the voice and throat. Be aware of how you use your voice in non-singing situations. The best vocal singing technique can be completely undone by abuse of the vocal cords and poor vocal speaking technique. Above all, stay well hydrated, all the time, not just when you are singing. It cannot be stressed too much: you cannot care for your voice without caring for your whole self.

Warming Up

If you were to get into your car on a cold February morning, back out of the garage, and immediately pull onto the expressway at sixty miles per hour, you would probably not be surprised to find that your automobile did not perform as well as it should. Nor would an athlete simply leap out of bed in the morning, swallow a quick cup of coffee, and immediately run a marathon. Yet far too many singers attempt the exact vocal parallel to these situations on Sunday mornings, especially at an early morning liturgy. You owe it to your instrument (and yourself) to prepare your voice for the work it needs to do, if you are to do it well and without doing damage to your instrument.[1]

Many singers are reliant on a bottle of water beside them at all times while singing. Often this reliance is due to the fact that they do not hydrate consistently, all the time, 24/7. Consistent and steady hydration should correct this need to sip water after every song, even in dry spaces.

Stretching

Stretch both arms over your head. Reach up very slowly with one arm at a time, as though you were climbing a rope ladder; feel the stretch down your sides all the way to your waist. From the same position, slowly reach your left arm sideways over your head to your right, as though making the "C" from the well-known "YMCA" dance. Hold this stretch for a few moments, and then return to center.

Repeat to the left. Gently shake out your arms and shoulders.

Drop your arms to your sides and slowly roll your shoulders. Take them forward, then up, then back, then down. Repeat this motion a few times, and then reverse. Drop your head down to the front (just your head; keep your shoulders comfortably upright and relaxed). Let your head roll gently to the side until your right ear is over your right shoulder, being careful not to raise the shoulders. Feel the gentle stretch down the left side of your neck. Let your head roll back to center front, and then repeat the stretch to your left, so that you feel the stretch down the right side of your neck. Repeat this back and forth several times. End with the head dropped to the front; inhale slowly, lifting your head as you breathe, and then exhale, staying upright.

Some people prefer to do these head rolls all the way around, first to the left, then to the back, then left, and finally forward again. This can cause discomfort to the back of the neck if not done properly, and the stretch to the back does not accomplish much more than the simple back and forth front stretch.

Take a few minutes to gently massage your facial muscles, concentrating especially on the cheeks and jaw. Stretch and scrunch your whole face a few times, to open up and release any lingering tension in these muscles. A gentle neck-and-back rub (self-administered can do a wonderful job if there is no one to assist!) to the neck and upper shoulders can work wonders for releasing tension to the face and head.

Obviously, only do these stretches to the extent you are physically able to do so, and stop if you feel any pain. Pain is your body telling you you're trying to do more than it's able to do. Listen to it!

1. While each person will have their own approach to warm-ups, the basic components will usually be the same: stretching, breath work, basic phonation, low-range singing, high-range singing, and mobility of enunciators.

Breath Work

The muscles of the rib cage and back, which primarily assist our breathing, also should be gently worked into action. Breathe deeply, either through the nose alone or through the nose and mouth together, feeling the breath fill your ribcage and expand it all the way down to your waist, and then slowly exhale. Do this several times. (For many experienced singers, this deep breathing can be combined with the physical stretching exercises, in which each enhances the other and a small amount of time is saved.)

Basic Phonation

Most singers, before moving into specific vocal warm-ups, will engage in some very simple and basic phonation, depending on their voice type. A series of gentle hum, sighs or "siren" sounds on a neutral "ooh" or "oh" vowel help to awaken the vocal cords and get them moving.

Low-Range Singing

Having access to a piano or keyboard is helpful for these exercises. Simple note patterns (such as the one below), sung each time lowered by a half-step, help to awaken the lower registers:

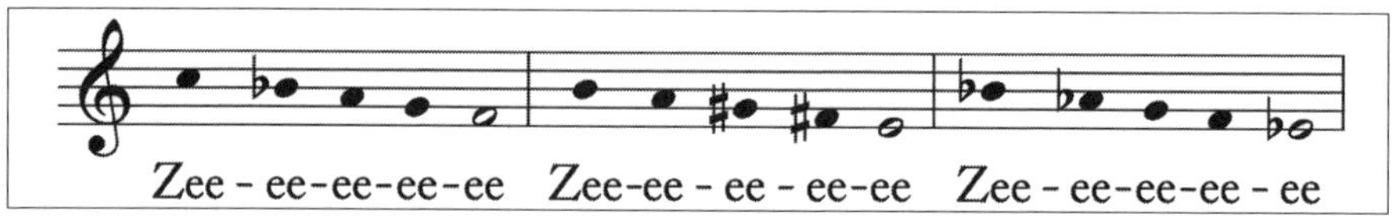

Proceed down by half steps, in a gentle neutral volume (do not over-sing, especially when waking and warming the voice), as far as your voice is comfortable; try to stretch your range a little as time goes by, but don't overdo! It also can help to vary the vowels you sing; generally when singing lower, it is easier to use the "brighter" vowels, such as "eeh" or "eh." Once you're well warmed up on an "eeh" vowel, try challenging yourself by singing the same exercise on an "aah" vowel, or in alternation.

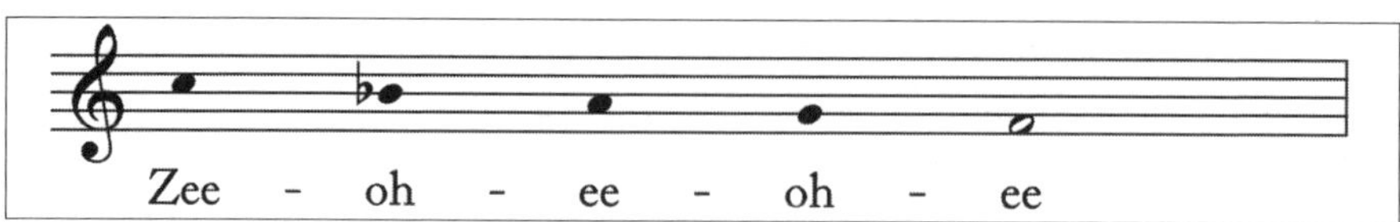

High-Range Singing

Just like the low-range warm-ups, singing some simple patterns on different vowels, ascending by half steps, can be a good way to awaken the higher registers of the voice.

As with the low-range exercises, while we do want to challenge ourselves to expand our range over time, we should not overdo. Singing to the point of pain or uncomfortable tension is never a good idea, and in warm-ups it is especially counterproductive.

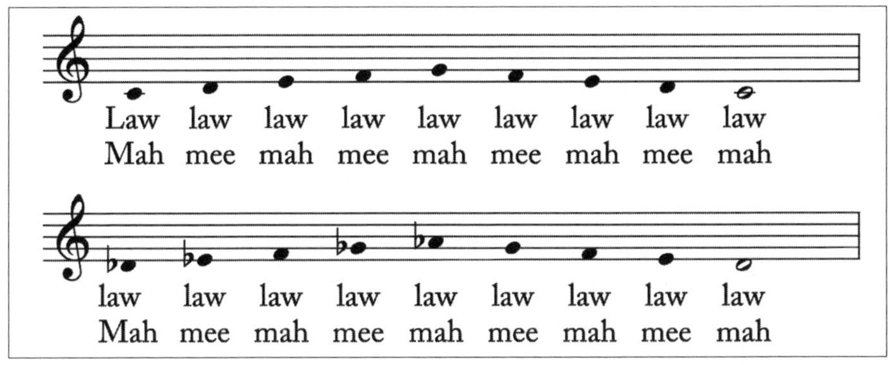

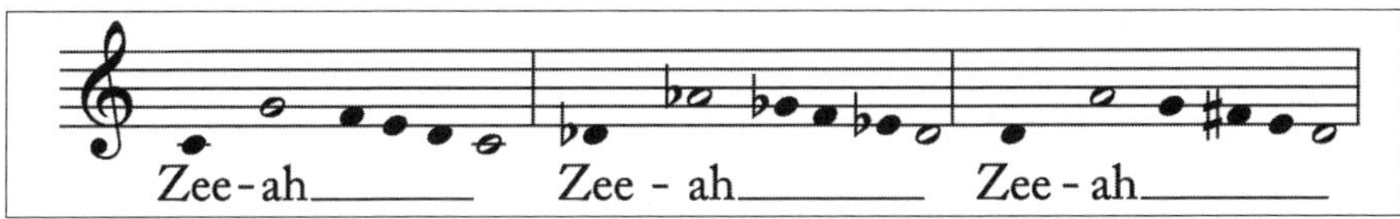

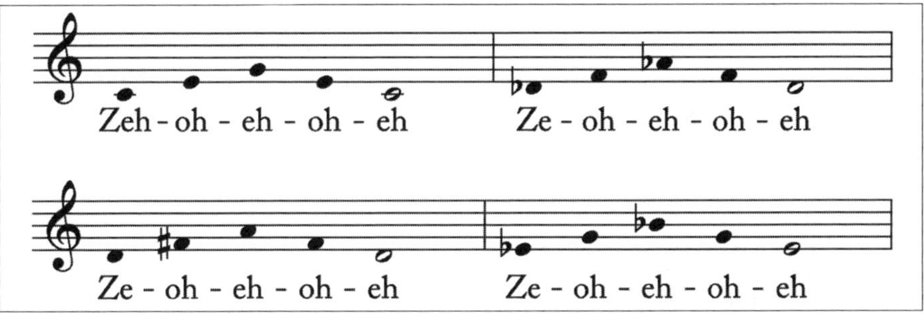

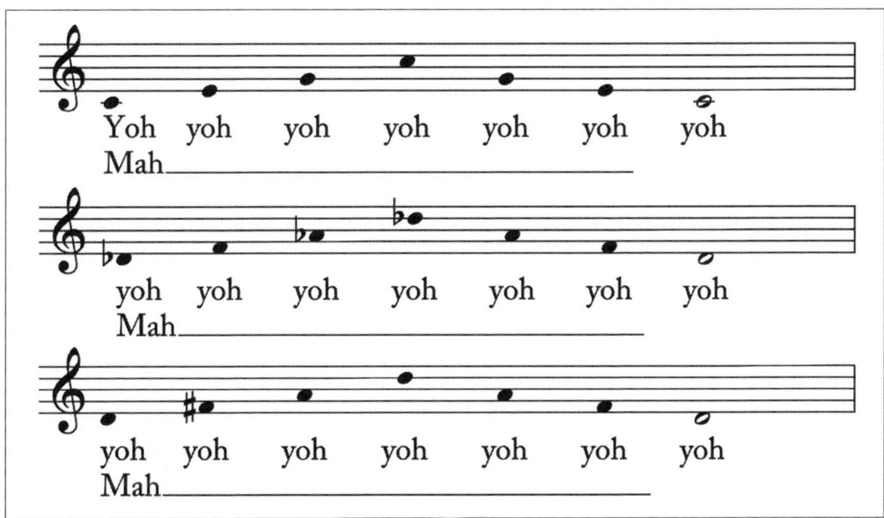

Resources

Church Documents

General Instruction of the Roman Missal: The introductory document, or praenotanda, that explains the theological background and gives the directions for celebrating the Mass. It appears at the beginning of *The Roman Missal* and is published separately.

Musicam sacram: An instruction promulgated from the Sacred Congregation of Rites (Vatican office) in 1967 that dealt with music in Catholic worship as envisioned by *Sacrosanctum concilium.*

Sacrosanctum concilium: The first constitution promulgated from the Second Vatican Council, this document forms the basis for our communal worship and includes sections on the participation of the assembly, liturgical inculturation, the Liturgy of the Hours, the liturgical year, and sacred music and art. It is often referred to by its English title, the *Constitution on the Sacred Liturgy.*

Sing to the Lord: Music in Divine Worship: Document issued by the United States Conference of Catholic Bishops, approved in 2007 and updated in 2012, that deals with music in Catholic worship. It addresses music as an integral part of liturgy, principles for the selection of appropriate music, and specific questions concerning music in the rites of the Church.

Pastoral Liturgy Resources

Budzkiak, Jennifer Kerr, Christopher J. Ferraro, Corrina Laughlin, and Paul Turner. The Liturgical Ministry Series: *Guide for Cantors, Third Edition.* Chicago: Liturgy Training Publications, 2021.

A theological, formational, and practical guide for training your parish cantors.

Foley, Edward, ed. *A Lyrical Vision: The Music Documents of the US Bishops.* Collegeville, MN: Liturgical Press, 2009.

A collection of four scholarly essays, examining the different documents on music in the liturgy from the time of the Second Vatican Council to the present. An excellent overview of how music in the United States Church has evolved, from *Musicam sacram* and *The Place for Music in Eucharistic Celebrations* through *Music in Catholic Worship* and *Liturgical Music Today* to *Sing to the Lord: Music in Divine Worship.* Particularly useful are the point-to-point charts that examine the different expressions of the different documents.

Funk, Virgil, ed. *Music in Catholic Worship: The NPM Commentary.* Washington, DC: National Association of Pastoral Musicians, 1983.

Another collection of previously published articles, this book takes each of the five sections of the US bishops' document *Music in Catholic Worship* one at a time; each section is printed in its entirety and then followed by four or five articles addressing the issues presented by each section.

Gelineau, Joseph. *Liturgical Assembly, Liturgical Song.* Portland, OR: Pastoral Press, 2002.

This book is essentially the collected reflections on the Catholic Church, assembly song, and liturgy written by one of the shapers of the Church and her song following the Second Vatican Council. Though somewhat scholarly in tone, this pastoral resource is eminently readable.

Gökçe, Diana Kodner. *Why Do We Sing: A Musical Guide for Catholics.* Chicago: GIA Publications, 2020.

A simple and straightforward guide especially for those new to the ministry, or even members of the assembly, summarizing the role of music in the liturgy.

Jordan, James. *The Musician's Soul Trilogy.* Chicago: GIA Publications, 1999, 2002, 2006.

Each book in this trilogy by renowned conductor James Jordan is like a retreat on paper, deserving of being read and reread, with quotes from musicians and others interspersed with Dr. Jordan's own reflections on music and music making. The three books include:

- *The Musician's Soul: A Journey Examining Spirituality for Performers, Teachers, Composers, Conductors, and Music Educators* (1999)
- *The Musician's Spirit: Connecting to Others through Story* (2002)
- *The Musician's Walk: An Ethical Labyrinth* (2006)

Truitt, Gordon E., ed. *The Way We Worship: Pastoral Reflections on the General Instruction of the Roman Missal.* Washington, DC: National Pastoral Musicians, 2003.

A collection of articles from "A General Instruction Primer" to items on liturgical catechesis, music, liturgical law, and pastoral theology designed to give ministers a clear, readable, easily grasped view of the *General Instruction of the Roman Missal.*

Ruff, Anthony, OSB. *Sacred Music and Liturgical Reform.* Chicago: Hillenbrand Books, 2007.

At nearly seven hundred pages in length, this thorough and well-researched volume of Church history and thoughtful analysis is not for the faint of heart—but it is full of valuable insights into the development of liturgical music through several stages of liturgical reform.

Vanni, Trish Sullivan, Paul Turner, and Joyce Donahue. *From Mass to Mission: Understanding the Mass and Its Significance for Our Christian Life.* Chicago: Liturgy Training Publications, 2016.

This series of booklets for adults, teens, and children provides a basic understanding of the Mass and our Christian call to discipleship. Individual leader booklets for adults, teens, and children.

Music Development Resources

For Singers

Breedlove, Jennifer Kerr. *Sight-Sing a New Song.* Franklin Park, IL: World Library Publications, 2004. *This resource is now available from GIA Publications.*

Designed both for classroom use and for self-study with a keyboard, this method gives a basic introduction to the skills of sight-reading and musical notation, specifically geared to the needs of the volunteer singer. Also now available in Spanish: *Aprende a leer la musica,* translated by Marieth Quintero, 2011.

Conable, Barbara H., and Benjamin J. Conable. *What Every Musician Needs to Know about the Body.* Chicago: GIA Publications, 1998, 2000.

Based on a six-hour course of the same name, this book explains an approach to healthy and efficient use of the human skeletal and musculature systems, known as "body mapping." This book relies on illustrations, diagrams, and charts to give a very clear and understandable explanation of the workings of the entire body.

Eustis, Lynn. *The Singer's Ego: Finding Balance Between Music and Life.* Chicago: GIA Publications, 2005.

An acclaimed singer and voice teacher, in this very personal memoir-like account of her own experiences, Lynn Eustis addresses many of the concerns unique to vocal musicians.

Ferris, William. *The Care and Feeding of Singers.* Franklin Park, IL: World Library Publications, 1993. *This resource is now available from GIA Publications.*

A collection of vocal exercises aimed at developing healthy vocal techniques for singers as well as honing listening and intonation skills within a larger group.

Jankowski, Bridget. *Body Mapping for Music Ministers.* Chicago: GIA Publications, 2016.

This book is an excellent and easily understandable introduction to body mapping, an approach to healthy and efficient use of the human skeletal and musculature systems. This book relies on illustrations, diagrams, and charts to give a clear and understandable explanation of the workings of the entire body and how this understanding can deepen our skill as ministers.

van de Graaf, Kathleen. *Winning Warm-ups for the Voice.* Domenico Productions, 1999.

A sixty-minute CD of vocal warm-ups for singers, enabling them to vocalize systematically through all parts of their registers without use of a piano. Available in versions for female high voice, female low voice, male high voice, and male low voice. A second CD, *More Winning Warm-ups for the Voice*, is also available as a ninety-two-page book titled *A Systematic Approach to Voice Exercises* (also by Kathleen van de Graaf). Refer to the publisher's website: www.domenicoproducts.com.

For Instrumentalists

Anderson, Marc. *Drums in the Church.* Chicago: GIA Publications, 2005.

A very basic but highly practical DVD introduction to playing techniques and rhythm suggestions for several different kinds of hand drums, including Latin American congas, Middle Eastern dumbek, and Irish bodhran.

Conable, Barbara H., and Benjamin J. Conable. *What Every Musician Needs to Know about the Body.* Chicago: GIA Publications, 1998, 2000.

Based on a six-hour course of the same name, this book explains an approach to healthy and efficient use of the human skeletal and musculature systems, known as "body mapping." This book relies on illustrations, diagrams, and charts to give a very clear and understandable explanation of the workings of the human body.

Gary, Roberta, and Thom Miles. *What Every Pianist Needs to Know about the Body.* Chicago: GIA Publications, 2003.

Using the principles of body mapping, this book and accompanying video are designed to aid pianists, organists, and players of any keyboard instrument in using their bodies in a more healthy and efficient way and to avoid injury.

Fisher, Bobby, and Bob Hatfield. *The Pastoral Guitarist.* Chicago: GIA Publications, 1989.

These two books are staples for the liturgical guitarist and keyboardist, outlining some of the basic issues specific to these instruments.

LaGiglia, Denise, and Anna Belle O'Shea. *The Liturgical Flutist.* Chicago: GIA Publications, 2005.

A wonderful method book, addressing the particular concerns of flutists playing for the liturgy, including music theory, flow of the liturgy, and playing from keyboard parts or lead sheets, and also the basics of posture, warm-ups, intonation, etc. While obviously intended specifically for flutists, many sections of this book would be invaluable resources for other instrumentalists also.

Other Resources

The Choir in the Liturgy: A Pastoral Music Resource. Washington, DC: National Association of Pastoral Musicians, 2006.

A collection of articles on aspects of the choral music ministry geared mostly for the music director or conductor; nonetheless, they are good resources for anyone involved in any way in a choral ministry and address balance, repertoire, rehearsal, and recruitment issues for children's and adult choirs.

Janco, Steven R. *Developing a Workable Repertory for Congregations from the Worship Works: Practical Guides for Liturgy.* Franklin Park, IL: World Library Publications, 2009. *This resource is now available from GIA Publications.*

This slim volume, only thirty pages long, contains a wealth of commonsense knowledge regarding a solid rationale for and approach to building a repertory (as in a stable body of familiar liturgical music) for parish song. Anyone responsible for selecting music for their parish should read this.

Muro, Don. *The Church Musician's Guide to Music Technology.* Chicago: GIA Publications, 2004.

A basic guide for the beginner, containing information regarding electronic keyboards, principles of MIDI use, microphone placement for ensembles, recording and sequencing, music notation software, and musical education and development. Gadget-heavy at times, it nonetheless is a valuable resource, not just for music directors, but also for the music ministers on whom they frequently rely.

Prayer Resources

At Home with the Word®. Chicago: Liturgy Training Publications, annual.

An annual resource providing insights regarding the Scriptures for Sundays.

Fragomeni, Richard. *In Shining Splendor.* Franklin Park, IL: World Library Publications, 2006. *This resource is now available from GIA Publications.*

Reflections and meditations on the *Exsultet.*

Hommerding, Alan J. *Blessed Are the Music Makers.* Franklin Park, IL: World Library Publications, 2004. *This resource is now available from GIA Publications.*

Unlike most other collections of prayers for music ministers, this book is specifically intended to provide immediately accessible, seasonally relevant, brief, and musically rewarding prayer services suitable for beginning or ending rehearsals or meetings. An invaluable resource!

Hommerding, Alan J. *In Holy Harmony: Prayers for Parish Musicians.* Franklin Park, IL: World Library Publications, 2009. *This resource is now available from GIA Publications.*

This collection includes many of the same prayers found in *Blessed Are the Music Makers,* in a simple text-only format and removed from the prayer service format of the original resource.

Joncas, J. Michael. *The Michael Joncas Psalter: Responsorial Psalmody for Cantor, Assembly, and Choir.* Franklin Park, IL: World Library Publications, 2009. *This resource is now available from GIA Publications.*

A unique resource containing lectionary-compliant settings of the common responsorial psalms. Their format is such that they can be sung a cappella, and the verses are composed to be sung by a cantor over ostinato renditions of the refrain.

Nowak, Michael. *Called to Be Your Song: Prayers for Cantors.* Franklin Park, IL: World Library Publications, 2010. *This resource is now available from GIA Publications.*

A collection of both seasonal and occasion-specific prayers written for those who serve in cantor ministry.

Trapp, Lynn, and Carol A. Leitschuh. *In Harmony with God: Choral Prayer and Preparation.* Collegeville, MN: Liturgical Press, 2008.

A collection of brief prayer services (including prayer, Scripture, song, and reflection) for each season of the liturgical year. The "Director Edition" contains all the prayers and music found in the thirty-one-page "Choir Member Edition," with an additional fifteen pages of vocal preparation material, both general and aimed at using each of the seasonal refrains to teach a particular choral skill. A useful blending of prayer and practicality.

Truitt, Gordon E. *A Pastoral Musician's Book of Days*. Washington, DC: National Pastoral Musicians, 2000.

Generally following the Roman calendar for feasts and memorials, this book includes reflections not only for those saints we would normally expect but also marks the birthdates of composers such as Praetorius and Verdi, as well as key people such as Charles Wesley and Martin Luther King Jr.

Music Organizations

National Association of Pastoral Musicians (NPM)
962 Wayne Avenue, Suite 210
Silver Spring, MD 20910-4461
www.npm.org

American Guild of Organists
475 Riverside Drive, Suite 1260
New York, NY 10115
www.agohq.org

Music Publishers

GIA Publications, Inc.
7404 South Mason Avenue
Chicago, IL 60638
www.giamusic.com
*World Library Publications is now an imprint of GIA.

Liturgical Press
Saint John's Abbey
PO Box 7500
Collegeville, MN 56321-7500
www.litpress.org

Oregon Catholic Press (OCP)
5536 NE Hassalo
Portland, OR 97213-3638
www.ocp.org

Glossary

Acclamation: A brief, joyful liturgical response, such as "amen" or "blessed be God!"

Agnus Dei: Latin for "Lamb of God." It usually refers to the invocation sung or spoken as the consecrated bread is broken by the priest.

Alleluia: Hebrew for "Praise the Lord"; an acclamation of praise. It is found in the Old Testament, particularly the psalms. In some translations of the Bible it is found as "Hallelujah" or "Praise the Lord." In Roman Catholic liturgy it is used especially during Easter Time and omitted during Lent. At Mass it is sung before the proclamation of the Gospel.

Antiphon: A short refrain, frequently a verse of a psalm, used as a repeated congregational response to a psalm. At Mass, there is a suggested entrance antiphon and a Communion antiphon; the response of the responsorial psalm is also an antiphon. In the Liturgy of the Hours, antiphons are sung or recited at the beginning and end of psalms and canticles.

Antiphonal: A way of praying the psalms in which two choirs (groups) alternately chant or recite the verses. Originally, the term referred to the singing of a brief antiphon by choirs while the verses were sung by one or more soloists. Antiphonal seating is an arrangement in which the seats of the assembly are divided into two groups that face each other along a central aisle.

Canticle: A hymn, particularly one taken from sacred Scripture, though not from the psalms. During Morning Prayer, the second selection during the psalmody is a canticle taken from the Old Testament, and during Evening Prayer, the third selection during the psalmody is a canticle taken from one of the New Testament letters. The Gospel canticles—the Canticle of Zechariah, the Canticle of Mary, and the Canticle of Simeon—are a feature of the offices of Morning, Evening, and Night Prayer.

Cantor: A liturgical minister who leads the singing of the assembly at a liturgy. The cantor may also sing alone, such as singing the verses of the responsorial psalm.

Chant (or Plainchant): A sung text that is an integral part of the liturgy, such as the entrance chant and the Communion chant. The term also refers to the actual singing of such texts.

Chant Notation: The precursor to our contemporary musical notation. Chant notation, also called "neume" or "neumatic" notation, has four staff lines instead of five; the shape of the note-heads (called "neumes") indicates the relative length of the note.

Choir: A select group of singers who sing during the liturgical rites of the Church. The choir supports the singing of the entire assembly and should not dominate or replace the congregational singing. Like all liturgical ministers, the choir is to facilitate the full, conscious, and active participation of all. Choir can also refer to a separate chapel where seats (choir stalls) are arranged so that one half of the assembly faces the other half, especially where the assembly prays the Liturgy of the Hours "in choir."

Communion Antiphon: A verse from sacred Scripture provided in *The Roman Missal* that may be sung or said during the reception of Communion at Mass. Originally, the antiphon was the refrain from a psalm that was chanted during Communion, which is still an option in the current missal.

Communion Rite: The portion of the Mass that begins immediately after the Amen of the Eucharistic Prayer and ends with the prayer after communion. It includes the Lord's Prayer, the sign of peace, Lamb of God, and the reception of Communion.

Concluding Rites: The last part of the Mass, following the Communion Rite. It consists of brief announcements, a greeting, a blessing, and the dismissal of the assembly. If an additional rite follows the Mass, such as the Final Commendation at a funeral or a procession with the Blessed Sacrament, that rite replaces the Concluding Rites of the Mass. The term can also refer to the closing rites in any liturgy.

Doxology: A hymn or prayer of praise to God. The Glory to God in the Highest, said or sung at Mass, is sometimes called the "Great Doxology," and the prayer "Glory to the Father, and to the Son, and to the Holy Spirit," used in the Rosary and the Liturgy of the Hours, is sometimes called the "Minor Doxology." Endings to certain prayers are also called doxologies if "praise" or "glory" are mentioned, such as the conclusion to the Eucharistic Prayer ("Through him, and with him, and in him . . .") and the Lord's Prayer at Mass ("For the kingdom, the power and the glory are yours now and for ever").

Entrance Antiphon: A text almost always taken from sacred Scripture that is sung or said at the very beginning of Mass, usually during the entrance procession. It is sometimes referred to as the *introit*. The entrance antiphon is given in *The Roman Missal*. Originally the antiphon began and concluded a psalm that was chanted during the entrance, which is still an option in the current missal.

Entrance Chant: Another name for the entrance antiphon or opening song.

Exsultet: The solemn proclamation of the resurrection of Christ that is sung at the Easter Vigil after the procession with the newly lit paschal candle. Ideally it is sung by a deacon, although it may also be sung by the priest celebrant, or a concelebrating priest, or a lay cantor. *Exsultet* derives its name from the first word of the Latin text, meaning "rejoice." The authorship of the Exsultet is unknown, but tradition sometimes attributes this great poem of praise to St. Ambrose or St. Augustine.

Gloria: The song of praise, which in English begins with the words "Glory to God in the highest," sung on certain prescribed days as part of the Introductory Rites of the Mass. It is based on the hymn of the angels at Christ's birth (see Luke 2:14).

Gospel Acclamation: The title given to the rite within the celebration of Mass that greets the Lord, who is about to speak to the assembly in the Gospel and prepares the assembly for its proclamation. The Gospel acclamation consists of the alleluia (or, during Lent, other words of praise) sung by all, followed by a verse (frequently from Scripture) sung by a cantor or by the choir, and then the refrain sung again by all. Several verses may be used to cover the action of a Gospel procession.

Gospel Canticle: The hymn that is sung or recited after the reading and its responsory at Morning Prayer, Evening Prayer, and Night Prayer. At Morning Prayer, the Gospel canticle is the Canticle of Zechariah; at Evening Prayer it is the Canticle of Mary; at Night Prayer it is the Canticle of Simeon. The Gospel canticles are treated with the same dignity that is given to the proclamation of the Gospel at Mass; hence, participants stand to sing or recite the canticle, and sign themselves with the sign of the cross at the beginning of each one.

Gradual: A name used at times to refer to the psalm sung or proclaimed after the first reading at Mass.

***Graduale Romanum*:** *The Roman Gradual*, the liturgical book that contains the chants of the Mass, along with their musical notation. Both the ordinary and the proper of the Mass are contained in this book.

***Graduale Simplex*:** *The Simple Gradual*, a liturgical book that contains simpler chants to be sung in place of the more complex melodies found in the *Graduale Romanum*.

Gregorian Chant: A form of chant, named after Pope Gregory the Great, that does not employ any harmonies. It has been used for centuries in the celebration of Mass in the Roman Church.

Hymn (Strophic Hymn): Musical form in which the melody for a verse is repeated several times with a different text for each verse, or "strophe" (for example, "Joy to the World").

Leader of Song: A function of the cantor. The leader of song is primarily responsible for fostering musical participation from the assembly through strong musical leadership, proper gesture, facial expression, and invitation.

Introductory Rites: The beginning of Mass or another liturgy. The Introductory Rites at Mass usually consist of the entrance procession, the Sign of the Cross, the greeting, the penitential act, or rite of sprinkling, the Gloria when prescribed, and the collect.

Introit: The entrance antiphon. In the Tridentine missal the complete introit consisted of the antiphon, a psalm verse, the Glory to the Father, and a repetition of the antiphon.

Kyrie, Eleison: Greek for "Lord, have mercy." It is an invocation used in litanies, particularly in the Introductory Rites, sung alternately with "Christe, eleison" ("Christ, have mercy").

Litany: A form of prayer in which a standard response is given to a series of invocations. In the Mass, the universal prayer and the Agnus Dei are both in the form of litanies. The Kyrie seems to be the response to a litany that disappeared somewhere in history. At ordinations, religious professions, and baptisms, the Litany of the Saints is prayed.

Liturgy: Any official form of public worship, from the Greek word *leitourgia,* "work of the people." In the Eastern Churches, the Mass is often called the Divine Liturgy. The title is frequently used in conjunction with a modifier, such as the Liturgy of the Hours or the Liturgy of the Eucharist. "The liturgy" is often used to refer to the Mass.

Liturgy of the Eucharist: One of two major sections of the Mass, along with the Liturgy of the Word. It begins after the universal prayer and ends with the prayer after Communion. It is structured around the fourfold Eucharistic actions of "take, bless, break, give," enacted in the presentation and preparation of the gifts, the Eucharistic Prayer, the fraction rite, and the Communion Rite.

Liturgy of the Hours: The official daily prayer of the Church, also called the Divine Office or the breviary. It is made up of the canonical hours of Morning Prayer, Midday Prayer (which consists of Midmorning Prayer, Midday Prayer, or Midafternoon Prayer), Evening Prayer, Night Prayer, and the Office of Readings. The hours are made up of hymns, psalms, canticles, Scripture readings, intercessions, and prayers.

Liturgy of the Word: One of two major sections of the Mass, along with the Liturgy of the Eucharist. It follows the Introductory Rites and ends with the universal prayer. On Sundays and solemnities, it consists of the first reading, usually from the Old Testament; the responsorial psalm; the second reading, from one of the New Testament letters or Revelation; the alleluia or verse before the Gospel; the Gospel; a homily; the profession of faith, and the universal prayer. On weekdays, only one reading precedes the Gospel, and the profession of faith is not prescribed.

Memorial Acclamation: The acclamation made by the assembly during the Eucharistic Prayer, after the institution narrative and the invitation, "The mystery of faith." Each acclamation refers in some way to the paschal mystery and the second coming of Christ.

Neume: Note-head used in chant notation.

Offertory Song: The chant that occurs at the preparation of the gifts.

Ordinary: Texts in the liturgy that change week to week based on the liturgical calendar. These include the readings from Scripture; the responsorial psalm; the entrance and Communion antiphons; and many of the presidential prayers.

Preface Acclamation: The Sanctus, which forms part of the Eucharistic Prayer and begins with the words "Holy, Holy, Holy Lord God of hosts."

***Phos hilaron*:** The major song of praise sung during Evening Prayer in the Byzantine Rite. It is a praise of God as the light of the world, and usually is sung immediately after the entrance of Vespers. It is usually translated as "O Gladsome Light."

Polyphony: Term that refers to two or more singers (or groups of singers) singing individual parts at the same time.

Praenotanda: The introductory texts in a ritual book, such as the *General Instruction of the Roman Missal*. Such texts usually have the title "Introduction" or "General Introduction" and provide important theological foundations and explanations for the ritual, along with norms, rubrics, and other instructions.

Prelude: A piece of music played or sung prior to the entrance song of a liturgy. It is not a formal part of any liturgical rites.

Proper: Those texts in the Mass and in the Liturgy of the Hours that are particular to a given day. The complete proper for Mass includes the entrance antiphon, Communion antiphon, readings, orations, and preface. The *proper* is distinguished from the *ordinary* and the *common*.

Psalm Tone: A simple melodic formula used for chanting the verses of psalms.

Psalmist: The liturgical minister who leads the singing of the responsorial psalm at Mass. Sometimes this role is combined with that of the cantor.

Psalmody: The section within each of the hours in the Liturgy of the Hours where the psalms are sung or recited. For some of the hours, the psalmody comprises only psalms; for others, the psalmody is composed of psalms and a canticle.

Psalter: The Book of Psalms itself; also the body of psalms that are used in the Liturgy of the Hours, and a book that contains all these psalms.

Responses: The answers made by the assembly to the various prayers, greetings, and proclamations of Scripture during the celebration of any liturgy.

Responsorial: The type of chanting, usually of a psalm, in which a soloist sings the verses while the choir or assembly sings a response, usually after each verse.

Responsorial Psalm: The psalm that is sung or recited after the first reading in a liturgy; also called the Gradual. It is normally proclaimed responsorially, with a psalmist singing the text of the psalm and the assembly responding with a response usually taken from a verse of the same psalm.

Responsory: The verses, usually taken from the psalms, used as a response to the Scripture reading during the celebration of one of the hours of the Liturgy of the Hours.

Ritual Music/Sacred Music: Any music that forms an integral part of the Roman Catholic liturgy.[1]

Seasonal Responsorial Psalm: The lectionary makes provision for certain psalms to replace the weekly "proper" psalms for those parishes for whom learning the entire cycle of psalmody would be too difficult. Several psalms are specified for use during different seasons of the liturgical year.

Sequence: A poetic hymn sung before the Gospel acclamation on certain days. Sequences are required on Easter Sunday and Pentecost; they are optional on the Solemnity of the Most Holy Body and Blood of the Lord and on the Memorial of Our Lady of Sorrows.

Song Form: Also known as "verse-refrain" form. Musical form in which verses of music (with identical melody but different texts) alternate with a consistent refrain (identical melody and text). Examples include "Remember Your Love" and "On Eagle's Wings."

Strophe: One verse, or stanza, of a strophic hymn in through-composed form: Term commonly given to pieces of music with no set repetitions or refrains. In the liturgy, this form is the Eucharistic acclamation, and sometimes the Gloria.

Three Judgments: Title sometimes given to the process set forth in *Sing to the Lord: Music in Divine Worship* for evaluating the appropriateness of a given piece of music for liturgy. The first judgment, the *liturgical judgment*, determines whether the music meets the demands of the liturgy and supports the liturgical action, thereby conveying the appropriate meaning of the liturgical text or action. Second, the *pastoral judgment* asks if the selection promotes the active participation of the gathered assembly in the mystery, and if it is appropriate to the age, culture, language, etc., of the assembly. Finally, the *musical judgment* ascertains whether it is a good piece of music technically and aesthetically, capable of bearing the weight of mystery.

Trope: A short series of words added to a title or a form of address, in an invocation. For example, in the third form of the penitential act, in the invocation "You were sent to heal the contrite of heart: Lord have mercy," the phrase "You were sent to heal the contrite of heart" is a trope.

Universal Prayer: The intercessory prayers in the celebration of the Mass, following the creed on Sundays and solemnities or the homily on other days; also called the prayer of the faithful or bidding prayers, and formerly called the general intercessions. It consists of an introduction, intentions and responses to the intentions, and a concluding prayer.

Verse before the Gospel: The acclamation sung before the Gospel during Lent that takes the place of the alleluia, which is not used from Ash Wednesday until the Easter Vigil in the Roman Rite. It normally consists of a refrain addressed to Christ sung by all, and an intervening verse, usually scriptural.

---

1. "Sacred music will be the more holy the more closely it is joined to the liturgical rite, whether by adding delight to prayer, fostering oneness of spirit, or investing the rites with greater solemnity."

Prayer for Music Ministers

Alleluia!

Praise God in his holy place;
praise him in his mighty firmament.
Praise him for his powerful deeds;
praise him for his boundless grandeur.

O praise him with sound of trumpet;
praise him with lute and harp.
Praise him with timbrel and dance;
praise him with strings and pipes.

O praise him with resounding cymbals;
praise him with clashing of cymbals.
Let everything that breathes praise the LORD!

Alleluia!

—Psalm 150